RICE BOWL RECIPES
Over 100 Tasty One-Dish Meals

When I started to work on "Rice Bowl Recipes: Over 100 Tasty One-Dish Meals," I thought of open sandwiches. The sandwich came into being when the 18th century English Upper House member, the Earl of Sandwich, ordered convenient meals of meat or vegetables stuffed between two slices of bread or a bun. Since then, the sandwich has developed, culminating recently in America, to the open sandwich. A variety of toppings are piled into a mountain on top of bread and served grandly to guests as a treat.

Surely, our piling the main dish on top of rice in rice bowls, is the same idea. In standard rice dishes such as Oyako Don, the individual delicious flavors of rice, chicken, egg and sauce match perfectly, yielding a deep flavor. It is unfortunate that rice bowls, with the exception of Barbequed Eel on Rice, are ranked in a lower class and not thought to be appropriate for entertaining.

This book introduces more than 100 dishes of Japanese, Western and Chinese style along with inventions to please the taste of any guest. Also introduced are the sets recently seen at City Hotel in Japan, which are suitable for serving guests. They consist of a rice bowl, side dish and clear soup.

If you rediscover the easy to make, delicious, nutritionally balanced rice bowls, I will be gratified.

Mineko Asada

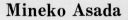

CONTENTS

Copyright © 2000 Graph-sha Ltd.
All rights reserved.
Published by Graph-sha Ltd., Tokyo, Japan
Translated by Lynda Ooka

Distributed by
Japan Publications Trading Co., Ltd.
1-2-1 Sarugaku-cho, Chiyoda-ku,
Tokyo, 101-0064 Japan

Distributed in the United States by
Kodansha America, Inc., through
Oxford University Press, 198 Madison Avenue,
New York, NY 10016

First edition, First printing: May 2000
Third printing: March 2003
ISBN: 4-88996-048-1
Printed in Japan

About the author: Mineko Asada has been a food writer for 30 years. In addition to her 50~60 titles, she works with food manufacturers in food development. With her extensive knowledge of cooking, her Asada Cooking Salon gives instruction in Japanese, Chinese and Western Cuisine.
Her various hobbies inspire her with great ideas for cooking.

Measurements used in this book:
    1 cup = 200 ml
    1 Tbsp (tablespoon) = 15 ml
    1 tsp (teaspoon) = 5 ml
Sake, Mirin and Dashi Stock are essential to Japanese cooking.
▶Sake (rice wine) mellows food, tones down raw taste or smells and improves flavor. Dry sherry can be a substitute for sake.

▶Mirin (sweet cooking rice wine) is used to improve flavor and give food glaze and sweetness. Mirin may be substituted with 1 Tbsp sake and 1 tsp sugar. Both sake and mirin are now manufactured in the USA.

▶Soup stock is made from chicken bones or meat. You may also use bouillon cubes.

▶For preparations of dashi stock, see inside back cover. You may also use commercial dashi stock.

Standard Rice Bowls

Ten Don, Una Don, Oyako Don, and Katsu Don are the four most popular rice bowls in Japan. Enjoy making homemade sauce to create your own family rice dishes.

▶ The suffix "don" is short for donburi, the bowls in which rice and toppings are served, and thus the meals themselves. Standard donburis have diameters of roughly 6~6¾″ (15~ 17 cm) and made of earthenware, pottery, or porcelain. Some come with fitted lids.

1 Chicken and Egg on Rice
(Oyako Don)

The name, Oyako, refers to the fact that chicken and egg are parent and child. Chicken and leeks are simmered in sauce, combined airily with beaten eggs and served over hot rice. Of the most popular rice bowls, the ingredients are most likely to be in the pantry and it has that casual feeling that fits like every day clothes.

Ingredients (1 serving)

3 oz (80 g) chicken breast

⅛ leek

1 egg

Sauce (refer to instructions at right)

1 serving rice

▶ **Oyako Pan**
A shallow pan with lid designed especially for Oyako Don, Katsu Don and other rice bowls. It conducts heat well and it is easy to slide toppings out of the pan and on to the rice.

The sauce determines the flavor

Dashi stock	Soy sauce
½ cup	1 Tbsp
Sugar	**Mirin**
1 Tbsp	1 tsp

Combine ingredients, bring to a boil. If you are making 4 servings, prepare 4 times the sauce.

1. Slice chicken and leek thinly on an angle. Bring sauce to a boil, add chicken and leeks. Boil thoroughly over a medium flame.

2. When the chicken is cooked through, pour the beaten egg along chopsticks to distribute evenly over all. When it comes to a boil, cover with lid.

3. When the surface is about half cooked, turn off the heat and place all, including the liquid, over hot, steaming rice.

2 Pork and Egg on Rice
(Tanin Don)

Pork bound together by egg on rice. The name refers to Oyako Don, that pork and egg are not related and so it is called Tanin Don (Stranger Rice).

Ingredients (1 serving)   2 oz (60 g) thin sliced pork loin / ¼ onion / 1 egg / Sauce (½ cup dashi stock, 1½ Tbsp soy sauce / 2 tsp sugar / ½ tsp mirin) / 1 serving rice

Method 1. Cut onion thinly. 2. Mix sauce ingredients and bring to a boil, add pork and onions. Simmer.
3. When pork is cooked and onions softened, pour beaten egg evenly. Cover with lid and cook over low heat until half done. 4. Place all, including liquid, over hot, steaming rice.

3 Breaded Pork Cutlet on Rice
(Katsu Don)

The original version of Katsu Don consisted of a pork cutlet placed on rice and covered with sauce thickened with flour. The pork cutlet is simmered in sauce and bound together with egg. In Okayama demi-glaze sauce is ladled on top (see p.12) and in Nagoya it is topped with miso sauce (see p.13.) Japan has a unique culture of Breaded Pork Cutlet Rice Bowls. Which dish do you prefer?

Ingredients (1 serving)

1 breaded pork cutlet
¼ onion
1 egg

Sauce (see instructions right)
1 serving rice

▶ To retain a crunchy coating on the cutlet, be sure not to simmer very long after placing in the pot.

▶ Pour beaten egg along chopsticks, little by little moving them around the pan to distribute. Even coverage results in a fluffy finish.

▶ Add mitsuba (honewort) leaves or green peas for color.

A slightly stronger sauce than for Oyako Don

Dashi stock	Soy sauce	Sugar	Sake
½ cup	3 Tbsp	1½ Tbsp	½ Tbsp

1. Cut onion thinly, add to pan with sauce and cook over medium heat until soft. Add cutlet sliced into ¾″ (2 cm) widths.

2. When it comes to a boil, pour beaten egg along chopsticks to distribute evenly. Cover and cook over low heat until half cooked.

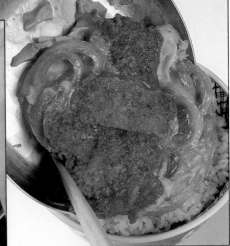

3. Turn off heat and slide out of pan onto steaming, hot rice.

To make pork cutlet

Ingredients (1 serving) 1 slice pork roast / Some flour and bread crumbs / ½ beaten egg / Oil for frying

Method **1.** Make slits in between the flesh and the fat of the pork with the tip of a knife. Gently pound with a pestle or a bottle.

2. Cover whole surface with flour, dip well in beaten egg and coat with bread crumbs.

3. Heat oil to 340~350°F/170~175°C (Bubbles will just form at the tip of chopsticks). Add prepared cutlet.

4. Spear with a bamboo skewer to check. When clear juice comes from meat, it is cooked. Finally, cook over high heat until browned and crunchy.

4 Barbequed Eel on Rice
(Una Don)

Barbequed eel was born about 300 years ago. Cut down the back to open, steamed without sauce (shiroyaki) and spread with sauce to grill, is the specialty of the Kanto region. Opened from the belly, and without any further preparation, spread with sauce and grilled is the specialty of Kansai region. Although both are called "Una Don", the way to open and way to grill are this different! To make easily at home, this book uses store bought shiroyaki (plain eel) adding a homemade sauce.

Ingredients (1 Serving)

2 pieces shiroyaki eel, store bought

Sauce (see below)

Grated wasabi (Japanese horseradish)

1 serving rice

▶ If shiroyaki is not available, buy frozen kaba-yaki (barbequed eel). Put pack directly into boiling water as directed on the package. Place on top of rice with sauce.

▶ Add wasabi according to personal taste.

Sweet soy flavor sauce

Soy sauce	Sugar	Sake/Mirin
2 Tbsp	1 Tbsp	½ Tbsp each

Mix ingredients, boil slightly to finish.

1. Prepare shiroyaki eel. (If frozen, let thaw at room temperature.)

2. Bring sauce to a boil in a small pan, add eel and coat well on both sides, Place eel on top of hot, steaming rice and cover with remaining sauce.

5 Eel and Egg on Rice
(Una Tama Don)

Eel coated in a sweet soy flavor sauce is bound together with egg. A soft, fluffy finish to the egg stimulates the appetite.

Ingredients (1 Serving) 1 skewer kabayaki (barbequed eel) / 1 egg / Sauce (2 Tbsp each soy sauce and water, 1 Tbsp sugar, ½ Tbsp each sake and mirin) / Some kinome (leaves of Japanese pepper) / 1 serving rice

Method 1. Cut eel into 1⅛" (3 cm) pieces. 2. Put sauce ingredients into shallow pan, bring to a boil, add eel and boil. 3. Beat egg and pour, distributing evenly. Cover and cook until half done. 4. Slip out of pan on to the top of hot, steaming rice. Arrange Japanese pepper leaves on top or flavor with powdered Japanese pepper.

6 Batter Fried Shrimp on Rice
(Ten Don)

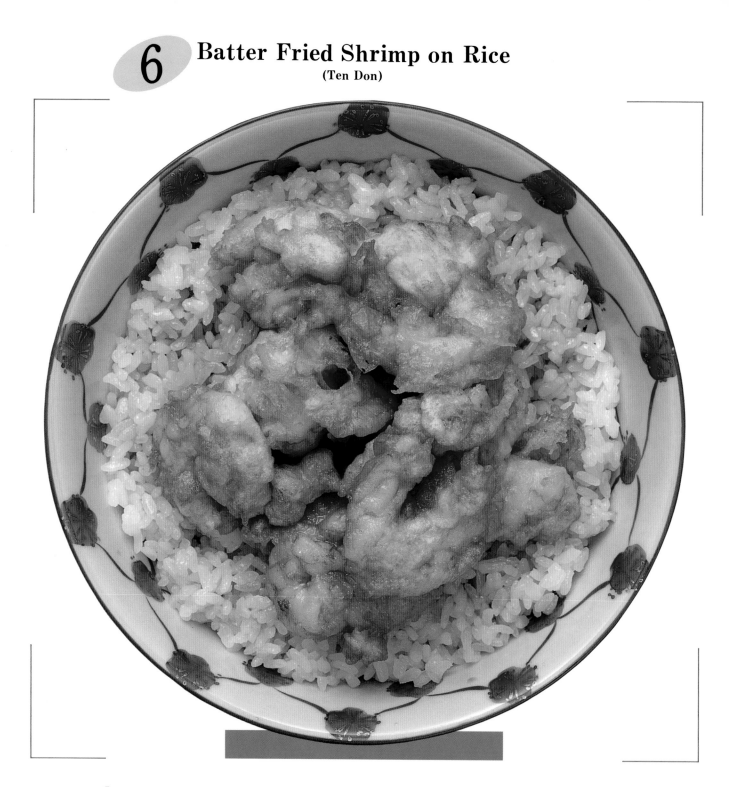

In this book, shrimp are fried together in batter, placed in a perforated ladle and dipped in sauce before placing on the rice to make a stylish rice dish. Also noted are soba noodle restaurant style Ten Don using jumbo shrimp, and vegetables and fried batter on rice, which is recently popular with women for being healthy and using ingredients on hand.

Ingredients (1 serving)

3½ oz (100 g) shrimp

Batter
- ⅓ small egg
- ½ cup ice water
- ½ cup flour

Sauce (see right)

Oil for frying

1 serving rice

▶ Devein shrimp, remove head and peel.
▶ Using a perforated ladle, dip freshly fried shrimp into the sauce and remove immediately to place on hot, steaming rice.

Ten Don Sauce is thick in flavor and texture

Add sauce ingredients to small pan and boil until reduced to ⅔.

Dashi stock	Soy sauce
¼ cup	2 Tbsp
Sugar	**Mirin**
2 tsp	1½ Tbsp

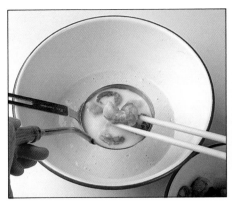

1. Scoop some batter (see below) into a ladle, add shrimp and gently stir.

2. Heat oil to high (345~355°F/175~180° C) and gently slip the ladleful into the oil. Fry until crispy.

3. Dip fried pieces in sauce, covering the whole and place on top of hot, steaming rice. Dish sauce over the top.

Making the Batter

1. Put the egg in a bowl, beat well, and add ice water.
2. Add flour by sifting through a wire mesh.

3. To prevent it from becoming sticky, use thick chopsticks and mix together half through.

Hints for frying oil

Using vegetable oil with a bit of sesame oil added, yields fragrance and flavor as well as a crunchy, well browned batter.

Variations of Ten Don and Katsu Don

7 Breaded Pork Cutlet with Demi-glaze Sauce on Rice
(Domigura Katsu Don)

Ingredients (1 serving)   1 breaded pork cutlet / 1 small onion / Sauce (¼ cup demi-glaze sauce canned, 1 Tbsp red wine, 3 Tbsp soup stock, pinch sugar) / Oil for sautéing / Some chervil / 1 serving rice

Method **1.** Fry cutlet as on page 7, cut into ¾" (2 cm) widths.

2. Cut small onion into thin rings. Heat up fry pan and sauté.

3. Put sauce ingredients in pan and boil until reduced slightly.

4. Place cutlet and onions on top of hot, steaming rice, cover with sauce and garnish with chervil.

8 Batter Fried Jumbo Shrimp on Rice (Ebi Ten Don)

Ingredients (1 serving)   2 jumbo shrimp / Batter (⅓ small egg, ¼ cup ice water, ½ cup flour) / Sauce (¼ cup dashi stock, 2 Tbsp soy sauce, 2 tsp sugar, 1 Tbsp mirin) / Oil for frying / 1 serving rice

Method   1. Devein shrimp, remove head and peel retaining the tail. Trim off the tips of the tail and squeeze out liquid. Use a knife to make two slits in the inner curve of each shrimp.   2. Make batter as on page 11, coat shrimp completely with batter. Place in oil (345°F/175°C) and fry until golden brown.
3. Place sauce ingredients in a pan and bring to a boil.   4. Place fried shrimp on rice and pour sauce over.

9 Fried Batter Balls and Vegetables on Rice (Agedama Yasai Don)

Ingredients (1 serving)   1 Japanese eggplant (⅓ American size) / 5~6 string beans / Some agedama (fried batter balls) / Sauce (¼ cup dashi stock, 2 Tbsp soy sauce, 2 tsp sugar, ½ Tbsp mirin) / Oil for frying / 1 serving rice

Method   1. Cut eggplant into ⅜″(1 cm) rounds and soak in water. Remove strings from the beans and break in half.   2. Dry eggplant between paper towels and fry to crisp in 345~355°F/175~180°C oil together with string beans.   3. Spread agedama over hot rice, top with eggplant and string beans. Bring sauce to a boil and pour over all.

10 Breaded Pork Cutlet with Miso Sauce on Rice (Miso Katsu Don)

Ingredients (1 serving)   1 breaded pork cutlet / 1 welsh onion / Miso sauce (2 Tbsp each sweet red miso and sugar, 3 Tbsp dashi stock, 1 tsp mirin, ½ tsp soy sauce) / 1 serving rice

Method   1. Prepare cutlet as on page 7, fry to crispy and cut into ¾″ (2 cm) widths.
2. Cut welsh onion diagonally and parboil.
3. Place ingredients for miso sauce in a pan, mix well and place on a medium heat. Stir with wooden paddle while thickening.
4. Place cutlet and welsh onions on hot, steaming rice and cover with miso sauce.

Soups

to Accompany Rice Bowls

Serving soups full of vegetables with rice dishes makes it easy to get a lot of vegetables and makes for nutritionally balanced meals.

Sawa-style Simmered Broth

Vegetable Miso Soup

Mushroom Broth

Vegetable Miso Soup

Ingredients (2~3 servings)   ½ potato, / 2″ (5 cm) celery / ¾ oz (20 g) string beans / 2 cups niboshi dashi (see inside back cover) / 2 Tbsp miso

Method   1. Remove strings from celery. Cut celery and potatoes in 2″ (5 cm) long thin strips. Destring the string beans and cut in half. **2.** Bring niboshi dashi to a boil, add vegetables and simmer slightly. **3.** Mix miso into broth, bring to a boil and remove from heat.

Sawa-style Simmered Broth

Ingredients (2~3 servings)   2″ (5 cm) each cucumber, carrot, and daikon / 2 cups dashi stock / ⅓ tsp salt / Dash soy sauce and pepper

Method 1. Cut vegetables into 2″ (5 cm) long thin strips.
2. Bring dashi stock to a boil, add vegetables and parboil. **3.** Add salt, soy sauce and pepper to flavor.

Mushroom Broth

Ingredients   (2~3 servings)   ½ pack enokidake mushrooms / 1 large edible chrysanthemum / 2 cups dashi stock / ⅓ tsp salt / Dash soy sauce

Method   1. Cut away the root head of mushrooms. Separate petals of chrysanthemum.
2. Bring dashi stock to a boil. Add mushrooms and chrysanthemums. Adjust taste with salt and soy sauce. Parboil and turn off heat.

Fried Batter Ball Soup

Ingredients (2~3 servings)   Some agedama (fried batter balls) / 2~3 pieces watercress / 2 cups niboshi dashi / 2 Tbsp miso

Method 1. Bring niboshi dashi to a boil, add fried batter

Fried Batter Ball Soup

Miso Soup with Sautéed Vegetables

Rolled Egg Soup

balls, mix miso with broth.

2. After simmering briefly, turn off the heat. Ladle into bowls. Trim hard ends of watercress and add.

Rolled Egg Soup

Ingredients (2~3 servings)   2 eggs / Some daikon sprouts / 2 cups dashi stock / Dash sake / ⅓ tsp salt

Method   1. Beat egg, adding salt to flavor. Pour into boiled water.

2. When it floats to the surface, ladle it out into cheesecloth, squeezing out the liquid to form a ball with diameter of 1″ (2.5 cm).

3. Lay on a bamboo mat and roll up to form a log. Cool. Cut into ⅜″ (1 cm) widths. Place in bowls.

4. Place dashi stock, ⅓ tsp salt and sake in a pan and bring to a boil. Pour in bowls. Trim roots from daikon sprouts and use to garnish.

Miso Soup with Sautéed Vegetables

Ingredients (2~3 servings)   ½ block tofu / 1 fresh shiitake mushroom / 3¼″ (8 cm) burdock / 1½″ (4 cm) carrot / Some kinome / 2 cups niboshi dashi / 2 Tbsp miso / 1 Tbsp oil for frying / Some vinegar

Method   1. Lightly drain tofu. Remove hard stem of shiitake and cut into thin slices. Peel burdock roughly and slice thinly on an angle together with the carrot. Soak burdock in vinegared water to remove harshness.

2. Heat oil in pan and quickly sauté the vegetables. Add tofu breaking it up and mixing while sautéing.

3. When all is coated with oil, add niboshi dashi and bring to a boil. Dissolve miso into broth.

4. Bring to a boil, shut off heat and pour into bowls. Garnish with kinome (leaves of Japanese pepper).

Rice Bowl Variations

The enjoyment of rice dishes is determined by how well the delicious rice, toppings and sauce complement each other. Japanese style dishes are a natural choice, but Western and Chinese dishes are delicious as well.

Seafood

 Scallops on Rice
(Hotate Don)

Ingredients (1 serving)   3 scallops / 1¾ oz (50 g) boiled bamboo shoots / Simmering stock (½ cup dashi stock, 1½ Tbsp soy sauce, 1 Tbsp sugar, 1 tsp mirin) / Some kinome / 1 serving rice

Method   1. Cut boiled bamboo shoots into thin 1½″ (4 cm) lengths.

2. Add stock ingredients to pan, bring to a boil, add scallops and bamboo. Simmer.

3. Arrange scallops and bamboo on top of hot, steaming rice. Pour sauce over the top.

4. Garnish with kinome.

12 Breaded and Fried Oysters on Rice
(Kaki-furai Don)

Ingredients (1 serving)   3½ oz (100 g) oysters / 1 tsp salt / Batter (flour and bread crumbs, ½ beaten egg) / 2 leaves cabbage / Sauce (2 Tbsp each Worcester sauce and soy sauce) / Oil for frying / Some scallions / 1 serving rice

Method   **1.** Place oysters in a colander and sprinkle with salt. Rinse under running water. Drain and press between paper towels. **2.** Dip oysters in flour, beaten egg and then bread crumbs, press lightly and place in 345 ~355°F (175~180°C) oil to fry until crunchy. **3.** Cut cabbage and scallions into julienne strips and toss in water to make crunchy. **4.** Place drained cabbage and fried oysters on hot rice. Mix sauce well and pour on top. Garnish with scallions.

13 Shortnecked Clams and Pickled Greens on Rice
(Asari Tsuke-na Don)

Ingredients (1 serving)   1¾ oz (50 g) shelled shortnecked clams / 1¾ oz (50 g) nozawana-zuke (pickled greens) / ½ knob ginger / **A** (½ tsp sake, dash sugar) / **B** (1 Tbsp soup stock, 1 tsp soy sauce, ½ tsp vinegar) / Some salt / 1 Tbsp oil for frying / Some red pickled ginger / 1 serving rice

Method   **1.** Sprinkle salt on clams and rinse under running water. Rinse nozawana and cut into bite size. Rinse again and squeeze water out. Mince ginger. **2.** Heat ½ Tbsp oil in a frying pan and sauté nozawana, add well mixed **A** and remove from pan. **3.** Heat ½ Tbsp oil in a frying pan. Sauté clams and ginger over high heat. Add nozawana. **4.** Add **B** to the pan, mix and dish over hot rice. Sprinkle with minced red pickled ginger.

14 Oysters Simmered in Miso on Rice
(Kaki no Miso-ni Don)

Ingredients (1 serving) 3½ oz (100 g) oysters / **A** (3 Tbsp dashi stock, 2 Tbsp red miso, dash each soy sauce and sake) / 3½ oz (100 g) spinach / Some salt / 1 serving rice

Method **1.** Sprinkle salt on oysters and rinse under running water.
2. Wash spinach well, taking special care of the root area making sure that no sand remains. Parboil in salted water, remove and cool in ice water. Firmly squeeze out moisture and cut into bite sized pieces.
3. Place ingredients for **A** in pan, mix and bring to a boil over high heat.
4. Add oysters and cook, stirring quickly over high heat until they puff up.
5. Arrange spinach and oysters on hot, steaming rice. Pour sauce on top.

15 Rice Bowl from Fukagawa
(Fukagawa Don)

Choose from a sweet soy sauce flavor or the original miso flavor.

■ **Soy sauce flavored** **1.** Wash clams in salted water, shaking gently and drain. Cut scallion diagonally. **2.** Bring **A** to a boil, add clams and scallions and simmer until the scallions are softened. Dissolve potato starch in double its volume of water and add to thicken. **3.** Turn off heat, add ginger juice. Ladle over rice.

■ **Miso flavored** **1.** Wash clams in salted water, shaking gently and drain. Cut honewort.
2. Bring **B** to a boil and add clams. When it comes to a boil, add honewort and ladle over rice.

Soy sauce flavored

Ingredients (1 serving) 3½ oz (100 g) shelled clams / 1 scallion / **A** (1 Tbsp soy sauce, ⅓ cup dashi stock, ½ tsp sugar) / 1 tsp potato starch / Dash ginger juice / 1 serving rice

Ingredients (1 serving) 3½ oz (100 g) shelled clams / Some honewort / **B** (½ Tbsp miso, ½ cup dashi stock, 1 tsp soy sauce) / 1 serving rice

Miso Flavored

16 Plain Simmered Conger Eel on Rice
(Anago no Shiro-ni Don)

Ingredients (1 serving) ½ plain simmered conger eel (store bought) / Shredded omelet (1 egg, pinch sugar and salt, oil for frying) / Sauce (1½ Tbsp soy sauce, ½ Tbsp mirin, 1 tsp sake) / Grated wasabi (Japanese horseradish) / 1 serving rice

Method 1. Beat egg and flavor with sugar and salt. Lightly oil a frying pan, add egg mixture to make omelet. Remove from pan, roll up and cut into thin threads. 2. Place sauce ingredients in a pan and bring to a boil.
3. Heat the plainly cooked conger eel and cut into 1⅛" (3 cm) widths.
4. Arrange conger eel on top of steaming, hot rice and pour sauce over all in a circular motion. Garnish with wasabi.

17 Conger Eel and Egg on Rice
(Anatama Don)

Ingredients (1 serving) 1 skewer barbequed conger eel (store bought) / Scrambled eggs (1 egg, 1 tsp sugar, pinch salt) / Some snow peas / Sauce (2 Tbsp soy sauce, 1 Tbsp mirin, ½ Tbsp sake, 1 tsp sugar) / 1 serving rice

Method 1. Cut conger eel into 1⅛" (3 cm) widths. Mix sauce ingredients in pan, add conger eel and thicken.
2. Beat the egg, add salt and sugar to flavor, put in a pan and turn on heat. Using 5 or 6 chopsticks together, quickly stir and mix to yield small scrambled eggs. 3. Parboil snow peas and cut into julienne strips. 4. Arrange egg on top of hot, steaming rice. Place conger eel on top and garnish with snow peas.

18 Barbequed Sardine on Rice
(Iwashi no Kabayaki Don)

Ingredients (1 serving) 2 sardines / Marinade (2 tsp each soy sauce and mirin) / 4 scallions / Sauce (1½ Tbsp soy sauce, 1 tsp sugar, 1 tsp sake, some ginger juice) / 1 Tbsp oil for sautéing / Some red pickled ginger / 1 serving rice

Method **1.** Dehead sardine. Open from the stomach and remove guts. Set in marinade for 2 minutes. Cut scallions into 1½"

(4 cm) long pieces.

2. Heat oiled fry pan, add sardine and fry both sides until well browned and crispy. Add scallions and sauté briefly.

3. Add sauce ingredients and flavor and thicken over high heat.

4. Arrange sardines and scallions on hot rice, pour sauce over in a circular motion and garnish with red pickled ginger.

19

Salmon Nanban on Rice
(Sake no Nanban Don)

Ingredients (1 serving) 1 cut of salmon (unsalted) / Nanban vinegar (⅙ onion, some carrot and green pepper, 1 red chili pepper, 2 Tbsp soy sauce, 2 tsp each vinegar and sugar, ¼ cup water) / Potato starch / Oil for frying /1 serving rice

Method **1.** Slice salmon on an angle and cover with potato starch. Add to oil preheated

20 Scallions and Tuna on Rice (Negima Don)

Ingredients (1 serving) ⅓ a block tuna (to be eaten raw) / 2 scallions / Seasoning (2 Tbsp soy sauce, 1 Tbsp each sake and mirin) / 1 serving rice

Method **1.** Cube tuna into bite sized pieces. Cut scallions diagonally into ¾" (2 cm) widths.

2. Place seasoning in a pan and bring to a boil. Add tuna and scallions.

3. Cook until tuna has changed color and pour all over rice.

▶ The name "Negima Don" comes from the ingredients. When spearing tuna and negi (scallion) with a skewer and grilling it is called "Negima Yaki" (grilled negi/scallion and tuna). When simmering fatty tuna with negi it is called "Negima Nabe" (negi and tuna simmered).

to high (345~355°F/175~180°C) and fry until crunchy.

2. For Nanban vinegar, cut onion thinly, carrot and green pepper into julienne strips. Remove seeds from chili pepper and slice into thin pieces. Place sauce ingredients, water and vegetables in a pan, bring to a boil and turn off.

3. Marinate fried salmon in the sauce until well seasoned, place on top of rice, add vegetables and pour some sauce over the top.

21 Doll's Festival Rice Bowl
(Hina-matsuri Don)

Ingredients (1 serving)   5 slices kamaboko (fish paste) / 4 Tbsp oboro (see below) / Shredded omelet (1 egg, pinch salt and sugar, oil for frying) / Some pickled rape blossoms, toasted nori, soy sauce / 1 serving rice

Method **1.** Beat egg, season with salt and sugar and make shredded omelet. (see p.19)

2. Sprinkle oboro over rice and arrange choice of kamaboko, pickled rape blossoms, shredded omelet and toasted nori cut into diamond shapes. Season with soy sauce.

Oboro (4 servings) **1.** Boil 3½ oz (100 g) of white meat fish, discard skin and small bones. Place in a dish towel and knead while washing under running water. Squeeze out water and place in a pan.

2. Add 2½ Tbsp sake, 1½ Tbsp sugar, a dash of salt, pre-mixed red food coloring and sauté over low heat using 5~6 chopsticks.

22

Shredded Tuna on Rice
(Tsuna Don)

Ingredients (1 serving)   1 can tuna (3 oz/80 g) / **A** (2 tsp soy sauce, 1 tsp each sugar, sake and minced ginger) / Shredded omelet (1 egg, pinch salt, oil for frying) / 1 knob small broccoli / Some salt / 1 serving rice

Method **1.** Drain tuna and place in pan with **A**.

2. Turn on heat and using 5~6

23 Shredded Salmon on Rice
(Sake Soboro Don)

Ingredients (1 serving) 1 cut salmon (thinly salted) / Dash sake / Shredded omelet (1 egg, pinch salt, oil for frying) / ½ sheet toasted nori / Some chervil / 1 serving rice

Method **1.** Grill salmon, discard skin and bones and roughly break apart. Place in blender with a bit of sake and blend to make soboro. (It can also be done using a suribachi - mortar and pestle.)

2. Beat egg. Add salt to flavor and make thin omelet. Roll up into a log and cut into thin strips to make shredded omelet.

3. Cut nori into julienne strips.

4. Sprinkle nori strips over hot rice and top with shredded omelet, and salmon soboro. Garnish with chervil.

chopsticks break into small pieces while stirring constantly. This will be enough for 2 servings.

3. Beat egg, add salt, make a thin omelet. Remove and roll into a log. Slice thinly to make a shredded omelet (kinshi tamago).

4. Parboil broccoli in salted water, remove and cool.

5. Arrange half of the tuna on hot, steaming rice. Top with shredded omelet and broccoli.

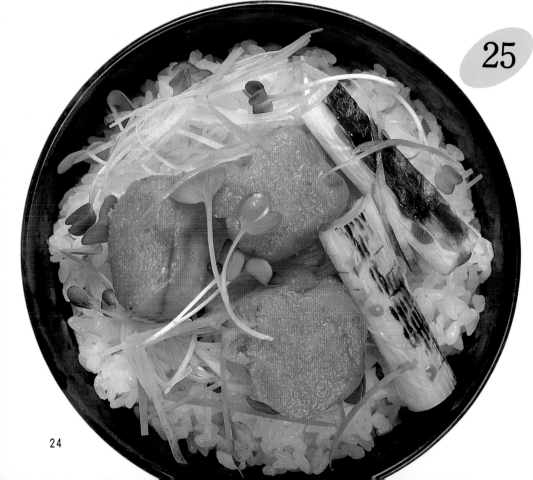

24 Horse Mackerel on Rice
(Aji Don)

Ingredients (1 serving)   1 horse mackerel / ½ cucumber / ½ tsp toasted white sesame seeds / Some daikon sprouts / Salt, Vinegar, Soy sauce / Grated wasabi / 1 serving rice

Method   1. Slice off hard portion on both sides of fish near tail, remove head and gut. Wash in salted water, wipe dry and butterfly fillet the horse mackerel. **2.** Sprinkle with salt and leave briefly. Wash quickly, dry and marinate in vinegar for about 10 minutes. **3.** Remove skin from head to tail, cut an angle into ¾" (2 cm) pieces. **4.** Sprinkle salt on cucumber and roll on cutting board to soften. Cut into thin rounds. **5.** Arrange horse mackerel and cucumber on rice, sprinkle with sesame seeds, and garnish with daikon sprouts. Pour 1 Tbsp soy sauce over. Garnish with wasabi.

25 Cod Roe on Rice
(Tarako Don)

Ingredients (1 serving)   1 pod mentaiko (hot, spicy prepared cod roe) / Some each carrot, daikon, daikon sprouts / ⅛ leek / Sauce (½ Tbsp soy sauce, 1 tsp sake) / 1 serving rice

Method   1. Cut mentaiko into 3 or 4 pieces.

2. Cut carrots and daikon into julienne strips. Soak in cold water to make crunchy.

3. Place leek on a well preheated grill and roll while grilling until toasted crunchy. Cut in half.

4. Drain carrots and daikon and scatter over hot rice. Arrange mentaiko and leeks on top. Garnish with daikon sprouts. Mix sauce ingredients and pour over in a circular motion.

26 Sea Urchin on Rice
(Uni Don)

Ingredients (1 serving) Some raw sea urchin / 1 sheet toasted nori / Sauce (1½ Tbsp soy sauce, 1 tsp sake) / Some cucumber and grated wasabi / 1 serving rice

Method **1.** Cut half a sheet of nori into ¾″ (2 cm) squares. Cut the remainder into julienne strips.

2. Place the ¾″ (2 cm) square pieces of nori on hot rice and arrange sea urchin on top. Mix sauce ingredients well and pour around the bowl. Garnish with shredded nori.

3. Cut cucumber into a decorative garnish, fill with wasabi and place on rice.

27 Raw Tuna and Mountain Yam on Rice
(Yamakake Don)

Ingredients (1 serving) ¼ slice tuna (to be eaten raw) / 3½ oz (100 g) mountain yam / 2 green perilla leaves / Aonori laver flakes / Grated wasabi / Some soy sauce / 1 serving rice

Method **1.** Slice tuna into ¾″ (2 cm) cubes, coat in soy sauce and let sit a few minutes.

2. Peel mountain yam and grate in suribachi (a mortar with grooves for grating). Add tuna and mix.

3. Place green perilla leaves on hot rice. Pile (2) on top in a mountain shape. Sprinkle with 1 Tbsp soy sauce and aonori. Add grated wasabi if desired.

28 Rice Bowl from Mito (Mito Don)

Ingredients (1 serving) 1¾ oz (50 g) hikiwari natto (fermented soybeans-crushed) / ½ small cuttlefish (to be eaten raw) / 1 egg yolk / ½ small green pepper / 1~2 scallions / **A** (1½ Tbsp dashi stock, 1 Tbsp soy sauce) / 1 serving rice

Method 1. Buy cuttlefish with skin peeled off for eating raw. Cut into thin strips, in bite sized lengths. 2. Remove core and seeds from pepper. Mince with scallions. 3. Place cuttlefish and then natto on top of hot rice. Make an indentation in the natto and fill with the egg yolk. 4. Scatter pepper and scallions around the egg yolk. Mix flavoring **A** and pour around the whole.

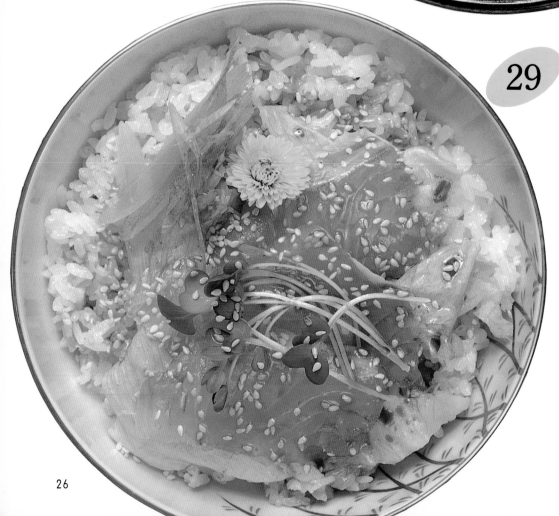

29 Raw Porgy and Vegetables on Rice (Tai no Sashimi Don)

Ingredients (1 serving) 3½ oz (100 g) porgy (to be eaten raw) / 2 leaves lettuce / 1 myoga (Japanese ginger) / Daikon sprouts / White sesame seeds / **A** (2 Tbsp soy sauce, ½ Tbsp sesame oil, 2 tsp vinegar) / 1 edible chrysanthemum / 1 serving rice

Method 1. Slice porgy thinly on a slight angle. 2. Wash lettuce and cut into bite sized pieces. Cut myoga into thin strips. Remove roots from daikon sprouts and wash. 3. Toast sesame seeds until fragrant. 4. Arrange lettuce and porgy on rice, and sprinkle with sesame seeds. Scatter myoga and daikon sprouts over and garnish with an edible chrysanthemum. Mix **A** well and pour around the top.

30 Cockles on Rice
(Torigai Don)

Ingredients (1 serving) 7~8 cockles / 1 sheet toasted nori / Marinade (2 Tbsp soy sauce, 1 tsp vinegar, some grated wasabi) / 1 serving rice

Method **1.** Mix marinade ingredients and coat cockles.

2. Cut ⅔ of nori into ¾″ (2 cm) squares and the rest into thin strips.

3. Scatter nori squares over hot rice and arrange cockles in a circle (as in photo) around the bowl.

4. Pour the marinade over the top in a circular motion and top with nori strips.

∗If desired use vinegared rice (see page 55) for a refreshing flavor.

31 Pounded Bonito on Rice
(Katsuo no Tataki Don)

Ingredients (1 serving) 3½ oz (100 g) bonito (to be eaten raw) / ¼ cup grated daikon / Some grated ginger and red smartweed / 1 green perilla leaf / 1 chive / Pinch salt and vinegar / 1 Tbsp soy sauce / 1 serving rice

Method **1.** Grill bonito on a well-heated grill, turning until the surface color changes.

2. Cool by pressing lightly with wet dishcloth. Sprinkle with salt. Hit the bonito with the side of a vinegar coated thick knife to tighten the texture. Slice.

3. Place bonito on hot rice and top with green perilla. Place lightly squeezed grated daikon and ginger on. Sprinkle with thinly sliced chives and red smartweed. Pour soy sauce over.

32 Luxurious Abalone on Rice
(Awabi Zeitaku Don)

A whole abalone in a rice bowl is the epitome of a luxurious rice bowl. A great dish for seafood lovers. Use plenty of butter and Madeira wine (a kind of white wine) for a more flavorful taste.

Luxurious Abalone on Rice

Ingredients (1 serving)　1 abalone in the shell / ¼ onion / 3 canned mushrooms / ½ red pepper / **A** (2 Tbsp soy sauce, 2 tsp madiera wine, pinch sugar) / 2 Tbsp butter / Some salt / 1 serving rice

Method **1.** Sprinkle salt over abalone and wash with a brush. Using a wooden spatula remove abalone from the shell. Wash well. Chop innards roughly and set aside.

2. Cut onion in ⅜″ (1 cm) widths, slice mushrooms thinly and red peppers with a rolling cut.

3. Melt butter in a fry pan, add whole abalone, sauté until cooked through, and remove from pan.

4. Sauté vegetables, mushrooms, abalone innards and add **A**. Reduce slightly.

5. Slice abalone on an angle into ¼″ (7 mm) wide pieces. Arrange along with vegetables on rice and top with remaining liquid from the fry pan.

Pickled Coltsfoot

Ingredients (1 serving)　1 stalk coltsfoot / Sweetened vinegar (¼ cup vinegar, 1 Tbsp sugar, pinch salt) / Some red chili pepper cut into rounds / Some salt

Method **1.** Sprinkle coltsfoot with salt and roll on a board. Boil. Remove to ice water to cool. Peel off skin and cut into 1⅛″ (3 cm) pieces.

2. Mix sweet vinegar well, add red chili pepper and coltsfoot to steep.

Vegetable Soup

Ingredients (1 serving)　Small amount of daikon, carrot, celery, broccoli, onion, potato or desired vegetables / 1 cup soup stock / Dash salt and pepper

Method　Cut vegetables into ⅜″ (1 cm) cubes. Simmer in soup stock. Flavor with salt and pepper.

Meat

 Curried Beef on Rice

Ingredients (1 serving)   3½ oz (100 g) cubed rib eye roast / ¼ onion / ⅙ papaya / 1 Tbsp green peas / 1½ cup soup stock / ½ Tbsp each curry powder and cornstarch / Pinch sugar, salt and black pepper / 1 Tbsp oil for sautéing / 1 serving rice

Method **1.** Sprinkle beef with salt and pepper. Cut onion and papaya into ¾″ (2 cm) cubes.
2. Sauté beef and then onion with oil. Add curry powder and sauté until fragrant.
3. Add soup stock. Bring to a boil, turn heat to low and simmer for 10 minutes. Flavor with sugar, salt and pepper and add papaya.
4. When it returns to a boil, add cornstarch diluted in 1 Tbsp water. Thicken and add green peas.
5. Ladle over steaming, hot rice.

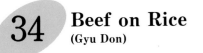

34 Beef on Rice
(Gyu Don)

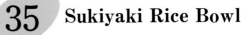

35 Sukiyaki Rice Bowl

Ingredients (1 serving) 4½ oz (130 g) cubed rib eye roast / 3 leaves cabbage / 1~2 scallions / Simmering stock (3 Tbsp soy sauce, ½ cup water) / Some red pickled ginger / 1 serving rice

Method 1. Boil beef for 20 minutes. Remove to a pan together with simmering stock. Simmer over low and slowly reduce.

2. Cut cabbage roughly. Cut scallions into ½″ (1.5 cm) widths diagonally, add to (1) and simmer 2~3 minutes.

3. Place over hot, steaming rice, pour some stock over the top and garnish with pickled ginger.

Ingredients (1 serving) 3 oz (80 g) sliced beef / ¼ onion / ¼ pack shirataki (devil's tongue jelly noodles) / 1 egg / Simmering stock (⅓ cup water, 1½ Tbsp soy sauce, 1 Tbsp sugar, 2 tsp sake) / 1 serving rice

Method 1. Slice onion thinly. Boil shirataki and cut into bite sized pieces.

2. Place simmering ingredients in a pan, bring to a boil. Add beef, onion and shirataki.

3. Place all on hot, steaming rice. Pour stock over. Top with raw egg.

36 Chinese Curried Rice
Use tonbandjan as a cover flavoring !

Ingredients (1 serving) 3 oz (80 g) thin sliced pork loin / ½ onion / Some green peas / ½ tsp curry powder / **A** (1 cup soup stock, 1 Tbsp soy sauce, pinch tonbandjan (chili bean sauce), oyster sauce, salt) / 1 tsp potato starch / 1 Tbsp sautéing oil / Some red pickled ginger / 1 serving rice

Method 1. Heat oil in a pan, add onions cut into wedges and pork. Sauté. Add curry powder·and mix.

2. Pour in **A** and cook over low heat for 5 minutes. Add green peas. When it comes to a boil, thicken with potato starch diluted in 2 tsp water.

3. Ladle over hot rice and garnish with red pickled ginger.

37 Steak on Rice

Ingredients (1 serving)   1 cut beef steak / ¼ onion / **A** (1 Tbsp vinegar, ½ Tbsp vegetable oil, pinch sugar, salt and pepper) / 2 sweet peppers / Sauce (1 Tbsp soy sauce, 1 tsp red wine, 2 tsp soup stock) / Some horseradish / Pinch salt and pepper / 2 tsp oil for sautéing / Some lard / 1 serving rice

Method **1.** Make incisions along the fat of the steak. Lightly pound steak and sprinkle with salt and pepper.
2. Slice onion thinly, sprinkle with salt and knead. Rinse. Marinate in well mixed **A**.
3. Make diagonal slits in sweet pepper and quickly sauté in 2 tsp oil.
4. Melt lard in a fry pan and cook steak to the desired degree. Cut into bite sized pieces.
5. Bring sauce ingredients to a boil and add grated horseradish.
6. Arrange (2)~(4) on rice and cover with sauce.

38 Three Colored Rice

Ingredients (1 serving)   1¾ oz(50 g) ground chicken / **A** (1 tsp each soy sauce and sake, ⅔ tsp sugar) / Scrambled eggs (1 egg, 1 tsp sugar, pinch salt) / ¾ oz(20 g) pickled nozawana (greens) / 2 tsp sesame oil / 1 serving rice

Method **1.** Place ground chicken in a pan with **A** flavoring. Over a medium heat, use 5~6 chopsticks together to break up and stir until it becomes tiny dry pieces (chicken soboro).
2. Beat egg and flavoring with sugar and salt. Place in a small pan and using chopsticks, as above, stir and break up to make tiny scrambled eggs.
3. Rinse pickled nozawana. Squeeze out water and chop into small pieces. Rinse again, squeeze out water and sauté quickly in sesame oil.
4. Arrange chicken soboro, scrambled eggs and nozawana colorfully on hot rice.

Grilled Chicken on Rice
(Kiji Yaki Don)

Ingredients (1 serving)   1 chicken thigh / Marinade (3 Tbsp soy sauce, 2 Tbsp mirin) / Omelet (1 egg, pinch salt, oil to fry) / ½ sheet toasted nori / 1 Tbsp oil for sautéing / 1 serving rice

Method 1. Cut chicken thigh in half. Pierce in several places with a fork to aid in flavor absorption.

2. Mix marinade, add chicken and marinate for 10 minutes.

3. Beat egg, flavor with salt, fry into omelet. Cut into ⅜″ (1 cm) wide strips.

4. Heat oil in a fry pan, add well drained chicken and fry both sides over high heat until crunchy. Turn heat down to low, add the rest of the marinade and simmer 3~4 minutes.

5. Place nori cut into ¾″ (2 cm) squares and chicken cut into 1⅛″ (3 cm) pieces on hot rice. Pour remaining sauce and garnish with omelet strips.

Pork and Scallions Rice Bowl
(Puru-puru Don)

Ingredients (1 serving)   3½ oz(100 g) sliced pork shank / 1 scallion / Pinch salt and pepper / Some worcester sauce / 2 Tbsp oil for sautéing / 1 serving rice

Method 1. Cut pork into bite sized pieces. Cut scallion in half and then into thin strips.

2. Heat oil in fry pan, and sauté pork over high heat until color changes.

3. Add scallions and continue to sauté well until browned.

4. Sprinkle with salt and pepper, and worcester sauce according to taste. Mix.

5. Ladle over hot, steaming rice.

Vegetables

41 Stamina Rice

Ingredients (1 serving) ½ bunch nira (Chinese chive) / 1 egg yolk / **A** (2 Tbsp dashi stock, 1 Tbsp soy sauce) /

Some white sesame seeds / Bit soy sauce / 1 serving rice

Method **1.** Parboil nira in a large pot of boiling water. Cut into 1½" (4 cm) pieces, squeeze out moisture. Sprinkle with soy sauce.

2. Arrange nira on hot rice, place egg yolk in the middle and sprinkle with toasted sesame seeds.

3. Mix **A** well and pour over top.

42 Rice Bowl from Tosa
(Tosa Don)

Ingredients (1 serving) 3¼" (8cm) daikon / ¼ pack daikon sprouts / ¼ cup bonito flakes / **A** (1½ Tbsp vinegar, 1 Tbsp soy sauce, ½ tsp sugar) / 1 serving rice

Method **1.** Cut daikon into julienne strips. Trim roots off of daikon sprouts and rinse. Dry roast bonito flakes, place in a plastic bag and knead.

2. Mix ingredients for **A** well, add daikon and daikon sprouts. Drain and cover with bonito flakes.

3. Arrange daikon and daikon sprouts on hot, steaming rice. Pour remaining **A** over all.

43 Eggplant and Beef on Rice
(Yanagawa-fu Don)

Ingredients (1 serving) 1 eggplant (½ American size) / ⅕ burdock / 1¾ oz (50 g) sliced beef / 1 egg / 3 Tbsp sake / Simmering stock (1½ Tbsp soy sauce, 1 tsp sugar) / 1 serving rice

Method **1.** Remove cap from eggplant and cut into 8 wedges lengthwise. Soak in water.

2. Peel burdock roughly and shave into slivers. Soak in vinegared water.

3. Slice beef thinly.

4. Place burdock, beef and eggplant flat on the bottom of a pan, sprinkle with sake and steam for 2 minutes.

5. Add simmering stock and simmer until burdock is soft. Pour in beaten egg. Turn off heat when it becomes half cooked. Ladle over hot, steaming rice.

44 Beef and vegetables on Rice
(Kinpira-fu Don)

Ingredients (1 serving)　1 green pepper / ¼ burdock / ¼ carrot / 1¾ oz (50 g) ground beef / Some minced ginger / **A** (2 Tbsp soy sauce, 1½ Tbsp mirin) / **B** (2 tsp soy sauce, ½ tsp each sake and sugar) / Some white sesame seeds / 1 Tbsp sesame oil / 1 serving rice

Method　1. Remove core and seeds from green pepper. Cut lengthwise in ⅜″ (1 cm) wide slices.

2. Peel burdock roughly. Shave into large slivers and soak in vinegared water.

3. Peel carrot and shave into the same large slivers as the burdock.

4. Heat oil in pan and sauté burdock and carrots. Add green pepper and sauté together. Season with **A**.

5. Place ground beef, ginger and seasoning **B** in a small pan, turn on heat and using 5-6 chopsticks break up and sauté until it becomes small pieces.

6. Arrange vegetables colorfully on hot, steaming rice. Scatter with fragrant toasted sesame seeds and place ground beef in the center.

45
Avocado and Crab on Rice

Ingredients (1 serving)　½ avocado / Some lemon juice / Some crab legs (boiled) / Sauce (1½ Tbsp soy sauce, 2 tsp sake, ⅓ tsp grated wasabi) / Some chervil / 1 serving rice

Method　1. Slit crab legs lengthwise and remove flesh and cut in 2″ (5 cm) lengths. Peel avocado and remove pit. Cut in half moons and sprinkle with lemon juice.

2. Arrange avocado and crab on hot, steaming rice. Pour over well mixed sauce. Garnish with chervil.

46 Pork and Eggplant Rice Bowl
(Nasu no Nabeshigi Don)

Ingredients (1 serving)   1 eggplant (½ American size) / 1¾ oz (50 g) thin sliced pork loin / ½ green pepper / ¼ onion / Seasoning (1 Tbsp sweet miso, 1 tsp sugar, ½ Tbsp mirin, 2 tsp soy sauce) / 1 Tbsp oil for sautéing / 1 serving rice

Method **1.** Remove cap from eggplant and cut on rolling wedges. Soak in water to remove harshness.

2. Remove core and seeds from green pepper and cut as for eggplant. Cut onion into ⅜″ (1 cm) wide wedges.

3. Mix seasoning well and put aside.

4. Heat oil in a pan, wipe moisture from eggplant. Add eggplant, pork and onions and sauté.

5. When all is well softened, add green peppers. Continue to sauté.

6. When the peppers turns bright green, add seasoning. Mix quickly to coat.

7. Place mixture on hot, steaming rice.

Eggs
and
Processed
Foods

47 Omelet on Rice

Ingredients (1 serving)   3 oz (80 g) can tuna / ⅙ onion / 2 tsp parmesan cheese / Egg mixture (1 beaten egg, ½ Tbsp milk, some granulated soup bouillon and black pepper) / Sauce (2 Tbsp tomato ketchup, 1 tsp each worcester sauce and red wine, pinch sugar) / Pinch salt and pepper / 1⅔ Tbsp oil for frying / 1 leaf lettuce / Some parsley / 1 serving rice

Method **1.** Drain oil from tuna. Mince onion. Heat 2 tsp oil and sauté onion and tuna. Add salt, pepper and cheese. Mix.

2. Remove to dish. Add 1 Tbsp oil to fry pan and heat. Pour well mixed egg mixture in. Use chopsticks to mix, making a large circle.

3. When half cooked, add tuna mixture to the front half and roll up.

4. Add sauce ingredients to a small pan and bring to a boil.

5. Arrange torn lettuce on rice and top with omelet. Pour sauce over. Garnish with minced parsley.

48 Fluffy Eggs and Tofu on Rice
(Fuwa-fuwa Don)

Ingredients (1 serving)   ½ block tofu / 1 egg / 2 Tbsp chirimen-jako (dried young sardines) / 1 Tbsp each sesame oil and soy sauce / 1 chive / 1 serving rice

Method **1.** Drain tofu. Beat egg well and mix in dried young sardines.

2. Heat sesame oil in fry pan. Add tofu and break up while sautéing. Pour beaten egg over.

3. Sauté until egg is half cooked. Flavor with soy sauce to finish.

4. Place on hot, steaming rice, sprinkle with chopped chives and add additional soy sauce as desired to season.

49 Scrambled Eggs on Rice
(Iri-tamago Don)

Ingredients (1 serving)   Scrambled eggs (1 egg, pinch sugar and salt) / ¼ green pepper / Some zaasai (season-ed turnips), salted kombu and red pickled ginger / 1 Tbsp soy sauce / 2 tsp sesame oil / 1 serving rice

Method   **1.** Beat egg. Add sugar and salt, place in a small pan and turn on heat. Use 5~6 chopsticks and mix to make scrambled eggs.

2. Rinse zaasai under water, cut into julienne strips, rinse again and drain.

3. Remove core and seeds from green pepper. Mince and sauté quickly with sesame oil. Add zaasai and quickly sauté together. Coat with soy sauce.

4. Scatter scrambled eggs over hot, steaming rice. Top with vegetables, salted kombu and pickled ginger.

50 Deep-fried Fish-paste Cake on Rice
(Satsuma-age Don)

Ingredients (1 serving)   2 deep fried fish paste cakes (Satsuma-age) / ½ pack baby bok choy / Some shimeji mushrooms / Simmering stock (1 Tbsp soy sauce, ½ Tbsp sugar, ¼ cup water) / Pinch salt / 1 serving rice

Method   1. Slice fish cakes into 2 on a slight angle. Trim roots from bok choy and parboil in salted water. Separate shimeji mushrooms from the root.   2. Bring simmering stock to a boil. Add fish cakes and simmer.   3. When well flavored, remove fish cakes from pan. Add bok choy and shimeji and simmer.   4. Place fish cakes, bok choy and shimeji on hot rice and pour the simmering stock over.

52 Grilled Aburage on Rice
(Yaki-age Don)

Ingredients (1 serving)   1 aburage (fried tofu sheet) / Some daikon sprouts / ⅓ cup grated daikon / **A** (1½ Tbsp soy sauce, bit vinegar) / 1 Tbsp soy sauce / 1 serving rice

Method   1. Cut aburage into 4 triangles. Trim roots from daikon sprouts and rinse.   2. Lightly squeeze out grated daikon. Mix with **A** seasoning.   3. Preheat grill well, place aburage on grill, baste with soy sauce and grill until crunchy.   4. Place seasoned grated daikon on hot rice, arrange aburage on top and scatter with daikon sprouts.

51 Zen Rice
(Shojin Don)

Ingredients (1 serving)   1 aburage (fried tofu sheet) / 1 scallion / Simmering stock (⅓ cup dashi stock, 1½ Tbsp soy sauce, 2 tsp sugar, 1 tsp sake) / Some red pickled ginger / 1 serving rice

Method 1. Pour boiling water over the aburage to remove excess oil and cut into bite sized pieces. Cut scallion on an angle. 2. Simmer (1) in stock and arrange on hot rice with pickled ginger.

How to Cook Delicious Rice

The success of a rice bowl is determined by the quality of the rice.
Please cook delicious, shiny, puffy rice.

POINT

1. Choose high quality, polished rice. Keep in mind the properties of regional rices and choose according to preference.

2. The quantity of liquid water should be 20% more than the volume of rice. (A bit less in the case of freshly harvested rice.) In summer, adding a bit of sake when cooking, yields flavorful, shiny, delicious rice.

1. Add plenty of water. Quickly remove any rice bran.

2. Next, throw away the water (taking care not to loose rice.)

3. Knead rice with the palm of the hand to polish.

4. Change water and wash repeatedly until water remains clear.

5. Place in strainer for 30 minutes. Add a measured amount of water. Cook.

6. Fluffy, shiny rice is finished.

Cherry Hued Rice Bowl
(Sakura-meshi no Donburi)

Adding easy ingredients, such as soboro and parboiled snow peas, yields a dish that is appropriate even for guests (see photo right).

Making Cherry Hued Rice

1. Wash 2 cups rice as described above, place in strainer and leave for 30 minutes.

2. Place in rice cooker adding 1 Tbsp each sake and soy sauce. Add water as usual and cook.

Chinese and Korean Style Rice Bowls

53 Tonporo Pork on Rice

Ingredients (1 serving)   4~5 pieces Tonporo / 1¾ oz (50 g) pea greens / 1 Tbsp soup stock / Some each sesame oil and salt

Method **1.** Make tonporo as below.

2. Rinse pea greens, heat sesame oil in a pan, add salt and sauté quickly. When oil covers all, pour in soup stock. Sauté until softened.

3. Place pea greens and pork on hot rice and cover with stock.

Tonporo (4 servings)   **1.** Place 17½ oz (500 g) boneless pork belly in a deep pan. Pound ⅛ of a leek and 1 knob of ginger and add to pot. Add water to just cover and turn on heat.

2. When it comes to a boil, reduce to low. Simmer for 40 minutes, skimming off any scum.

3. Remove from pot. Baste in 1 Tbsp soy sauce and fry in 390°F (200°C) oil until the color turns brown.

4. Slice fried meat into ¾" (2 cm) pieces and put in a bowl. Mix 2 cups soup stock, 3 Tbsp soy sauce, 2 Tbsp sugar, 1 Tbsp sake and add to bowl. Add 1 crushed star anise and ½ tsp Japanese peppercorns and steam for 3 hours.

5. Take out meat. Strain liquid and thicken with potato starch diluted in water.

55 Korean Barbeque Rice Bowl
(Yaki-niku Don)

Ingredients (1 serving)   3½ oz (100 g) thin sliced pork loin roast / ¼ tomato / Some salad greens / Marinade (1 knob ginger, grated; 1 clove garlic, grated; 1½ Tbsp soy sauce; 1 tsp sake) / 1 Tbsp oil for sautéing / 1 serving rice

Method **1.** Mix marinade well and soak meat for 5 minutes.

2. Cut tomato into half moons. Tear salad greens into easy to eat pieces.

3. Heat oil in a wok, dry moisture from meat and sauté both sides.

4. When it becomes browned and crunchy, add remaining marinade, turn heat to high and coat.

5. Place meat with its juices on hot, steaming rice. Arrange tomatoes and salad greens colorfully.

54 Beef with Oyster Sauce Rice Bowl

Ingredients (1 serving)   3 oz (80 g) cubed beef / 1 scallion / 4″ (10 cm) thin celery / 6~7 straw mushrooms, canned / Seasoning (1 Tbsp oyster sauce, 1 tsp each soy sauce and sake, ¼ cup soup stock) / 1 tsp potato starch / 1 Tbsp oil for sautéing / 1 serving rice

Method   **1.** Buy cubed beef for making curry, cut into ¾″ (2 cm) cubes.

2. Cut scallion on an angle into 1⅛″ (3 cm) slices and celery into 1⅛″ (3 cm) lengths, then in half lengthwise.

3. Mix seasoning.

4. Heat oil in a pan and sauté beef.

5. When beef is browned, add vegetables and sauté well. Add straw mushrooms and mix together.

6. Add seasoning. When it comes to a boil, add potato starch diluted in 2 tsp water to thicken.

7. Ladle over hot, steaming rice.

57 Eight Treasured Vegetables Rice Bowl (Happosai Don)

Ingredients (1 serving)   2~3 shrimp / 2 boiled arrowhead bulb / 2 oz (60 g) bamboo shoots / 3 straw mushrooms, canned / 1 fresh shiitake / 1 scallion / 1¾ oz (50 g) thin sliced pork loin / Seasoning (½ cup soup stock, 1 tsp soy sauce, pinch salt and sugar) / Sake / 3 tsp potato starch / 1 Tbsp oil for sautéing / Sesame oil / 1 serving rice

Method 1. Remove innards and shell shrimp. Coat with sake and 1 tsp potato starch. Parboil. **2.** Cut arrowhead bulb thinly, bamboo shoots into rectangles, straw mushrooms in half, shiitake on an angle in strips and scallion into ⅜″ (1 cm) wide rounds. **3.** Heat oil in wok, sauté pork and scallions well. Add vegetables and shrimp and continue to sauté. **4.** Mix seasoning, add to wok and bring to a boil. Add 2 tsp starch diluted in 4 tsp water, to thicken. Lastly, add sesame oil to flavor. **5.** Ladle over rice.

56 Chinese Beef on Rice

Ingredients (1 serving)   3 oz (80 g) sliced beef / 1 oz (30 g) shimeji mushrooms / 1 handful baby bok choy / Seasoning (⅓ cup soup stock, 1 Tbsp soy sauce, 1 tsp sake, pinch sugar, ½ tsp oyster sauce) / 1 Tbsp oil for sautéing / 2 tsp potato starch / 1 serving rice

Method 1. Cut beef into bite sized pieces. **2.** Cut hard end off of shimeji and separate. Remove root end of bok choy and cut into 2″ (5 cm) pieces. **3.** Mix seasoning well. **4.** Spread oil evenly in wok and heat, sauté beef over high heat until the color changes. **5.** Add shimeji and bok choy and sauté together. When softened, pour in seasoning. **6.** When it comes to a boil, add potato starch diluted in 4 tsp water. Quickly mix all together and thicken. **7.** Ladle over hot, steaming rice.

59 Spareribs on Rice

Ingredients (1 serving) 4 spareribs / Marinade (1½ Tbsp soy sauce, pinch sugar; ½ clove garlic, grated; 1 Tbsp grated onion) / Some scallions, tomato and cilantro / Sauce (1 Tbsp soy sauce, 1 tsp mirin, ½ Tbsp sake) / 1 serving rice

Method **1.** Mix marinade well and soak spareribs for 1 hour.

2. Line spareribs up in toaster oven and cook on medium heat for 30 minutes. (Or heat a pinch of oil in a fry pan, sauté until browned, then cook over low until cooked through to the middle.)

3. Cut scallions into julienne strips and tomato into thin half moons.

4. Bring sauce ingredients to a boil in a pan.

5. Scatter scallions over hot, steaming rice, top with spareribs. Garnish with tomato and cilantro. Pour sauce over.

58 Ground Meat Rice Bowl
(Niku Soboro Don)

Ingredients (1 serving) 3½ oz (100 g) ground pork / ¾ oz (20 g) zaasai (seasoned turnip) / 1 dried shiitake mushroom / 1 Tbsp scallion, minced / Seasoning (1½ Tbsp soy sauce, 1 Tbsp sake, ½ tsp miso, pinch sugar and chili bean sauce) / 1½ Tbsp oil for frying / Some red leaf lettuce and red pepper / 1 serving rice

Method **1.** Rinse zaasai well. Soak shiitake in water until softened, remove end of stem, and chop together roughly.

2. Mix seasoning well and set aside.

3. Spread oil evenly in wok and heat. Stir fry scallions and pork well.

4. When the meat flakes, add zaasai and shiitake, and continue to stir fry. Add seasoning, turn to high heat and flavor all for meat soboro.

5. Arrange torn, red lettuce on hot rice. Ladle meat over and garnish with rings of red peppers.

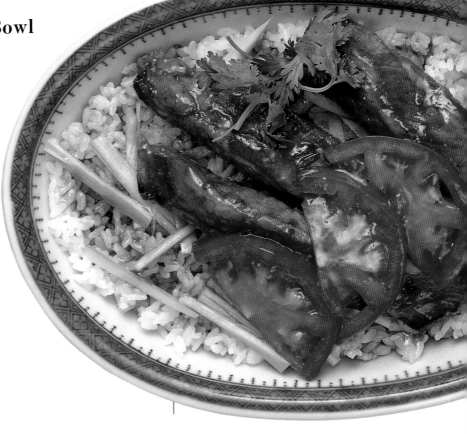

61 Tofu and Pork Rice Bowl
(Mabo-dofu Don)

Ingredients (1 serving)   1¾ oz (50 g) ground pork / ⅓ block tofu / Some scallions and ginger / Seasoning (1 Tbsp soy sauce, ⅔ tsp each red miso and sake, bit chili bean sauce, ½ cup soup stock, 1 tsp potato starch) / 1 Tbsp oil for frying / Some chives / 1 serving rice

Method **1.** Cut tofu into ⅜″ (1 cm) squares, mince scallions and ginger.

2. Mix seasoning well and set aside.

3. Spread oil evenly in a wok and heat. Quickly stir fry scallions and ginger until fragrant.

4. Add ground pork, stir frying until it separates into flakes.

5. Pour seasoning in, while stirring in add tofu. Let boil for 1 minute.

6. Ladle over hot, steaming rice and scatter chives cut in rings on top.

60 Flavored Bamboo Rice Bowl
(Menma Don)

Ingredients (1 serving)   3½ oz (100 g) water packed menma (flavored bamboo) / 3½ oz (100 g) ground pork / 1 Tbsp scallion, minced / 1 tsp ginger, minced / Seasoning (2 Tbsp each soy sauce and sake, pinch sugar, ¼ cup soup stock) / Some green peas / 1 Tbsp oil for sautéing / 1 serving rice

Method   **1.** Cut menma into uniform lengths and widths.

2. Mix seasoning ingredients together well.

3. Spread oil evenly in wok and heat. Stir fry scallions and ginger until fragrant.

4. Add ground pork and stir fry until it separates into individual pieces.

5. Add menma and stir fry together. Pour in seasoning and simmer 7~8 minutes. When done, scatter peas in.

6. Ladle over hot, steaming rice.

63 Crab Omelet Rice Bowl
(Kani Tama Don)

Ingredients (1 serving) Some canned crab / Some boiled bamboo shoots and scallions / 1 large egg / Glaze (⅓ cup soup stock, ½ tsp soy sauce, ¼ tsp sugar, dash vinegar, 1 tsp potato starch) / Some canned green peas / Pinch salt and ginger juice / 1 Tbsp oil for frying / 1 serving rice

Method **1.** Separate pieces of crab. Remove thin, clear bone. **2.** Cut bamboo shoot and scallions into julienne strips. **3.** Beat egg, mix in crab and vegetables. Season with salt. **4.** Spread oil evenly in a wok and heat. Pour in egg mixture. When half cooked, form a circle and turn over. **5.** Place ingredients for glaze in a small pan, bring to a boil and thicken. Mix in green peas. **6.** Place crab and egg on rice, top with glaze, sprinkle ginger juice to flavor.

62 Shrimp Omelet Rice Bowl
(Ebi Tama Don)

Ingredients (1 serving) 3 oz (80 g) shelled shrimp / Some mitsuba (honewort) / 1 large egg / Glaze (⅓ cup soup stock, 2 tsp soy sauce, 1 tsp sake, ⅓ tsp sugar, ½ tsp potato starch) / 1 tsp sake / Pinch salt and ginger juice / 1 Tbsp oil for frying / 1 serving rice

Method **1.** Coat shrimp in mixture of sake and ginger juice.
2. Cut honewort roughly. Beat egg and add salt to flavor.
3. Spread oil evenly in wok and heat. Quickly stir fry shrimp.
4. Pour egg into wok and mix, sprinkle with honewort. When half cooked, form a circle and flip over.
5. Place ingredients for glaze in a pan, turn on heat, stirring constantly to thicken.
6. Place shrimp and egg on rice and pour glaze over.

65 Chinese Pork on Rice
(Chuka Buta-niku Don)

Ingredients (1 serving)   1¾ oz (50 g) thin sliced pork loin / Marinade (1 tsp soy sauce) / ½ green pepper / 1 oz (30 g) each, boiled bamboo shoots, shimeji mushrooms / Some carrots / 1 leaf Chinese cabbage / Some soybean sprouts / Seasoning (⅔ cup soup stock, ½ Tbsp sake, ¼ tsp salt, bit ginger juice) / ½ Tbsp potato starch / 1½ Tbsp oil for sautéing / 1 serving rice

Method **1.** Coat pork with soy sauce. **2.** Cut green pepper and bamboo shoots into wedges, carrots into thin rectangles, and Chinese cabbage on the crossgrain into chunks. Cut hard end off of shimeji. Rinse soybean sprouts under water and drain. **3.** Heat oil in wok and sauté pork well. Add green pepper, carrot and Chinese cabbage and sauté to mix. **4.** Add remaining vegetables and sauté quickly. Add seasoning and bring to a boil. **5.** Pour in starch diluted in 1 Tbsp water to thicken and ladle over rice.

64 Shrimp Simmered in Tomato on Rice

Ingredients (1 serving)   5 shrimp / Some scallions and ginger / **A** (½ tsp each sake and ginger juice, 1 tsp potato starch) / Seasoning (¼ cup soup stock, 1 Tbsp each tomato puree and tomato ketchup, 1 tsp each soy sauce and sake, bit oyster sauce) / 1 Tbsp oil for sautéing / 1 serving rice

Method **1.** Remove innards and shell from shrimp, open from the back and marinate in **A**.

2. Mince scallions and ginger.

3. Mix seasoning well and set aside.

4. Heat oil in a pan and sauté shrimp. When they turn red, add (2) and mix.

5. Add seasoning and bring to a boil.

6. Ladle over hot, steaming rice.

66 Crab and Yellow Scallions on Rice

Ingredients (1 serving) Some crab (canned) / 1 oz (30 g) yellow scallions / Some green scallions / **A** (1 Tbsp light soy sauce, ½ Tbsp Lao Jiu (Chinese rice wine) / 1 Tbsp oil for stir frying / 1 serving rice

Method **1.** Remove crab from can and pull apart roughly. Remove the soft bone inside.

2. Cut yellow scallions into 1½″ (4 cm) pieces, cut green scallions on an angle.

3. Spread oil evenly in a wok and heat, stir fry yellow scallion and green scallions until soft.

4. Add crab and mix, add **A** and coat the flavor over all. Ladle over hot, steaming rice.

Bitingly Spicy Korean Style

67 Bibinba and Beef Rice Bowl

Ingredients (1 serving) 1¾ oz (50 g) each, soybean sprouts, zenmai, spinach, and ground beef / 1¾ oz (50 g) daikon and carrot, mixed / **A** (1 tsp light soy sauce, some each powdered red chili pepper and salt) / **B** (2 tsp soy sauce, 1 tsp sake, ½ tsp sugar) / Sweet vinegar (¼ cup vinegar, 2 Tbsp sugar, pinch salt) / **C** (½ Tbsp soy sauce, 1 tsp sake, pinch sugar) / Some powdered red chili pepper / Salt and pepper / Some each minced scallions and white sesame seeds / 1⅔ Tbsp sesame oil / 1 tsp oil for sautéing / 1 serving rice

Method **1.** Wash sprouts and sauté in 1 tsp sesame oil. Season with **A**. Cut zenmai into bite size and sauté with 1 tsp sesame oil. Season with **B**.

2. Wash spinach and cut in half. Sauté in 1 Tbsp sesame oil. Season with salt and pepper. **3.** Cut daikon and carrots into long thin strips, sprinkle with salt. Squeeze out water and marinate in sweet vinegar. Sprinkle with red chili pepper. **4.** Sauté beef. Add **C**, sauté and simmer until liquid evaporates. **5.** Place (4) on rice and arrange (1)~(3) on as well. Sprinkle minced scallions soaked in water and toasted sesame seeds.

68 Kimchee Rice Bowl

Ingredients (1 serving) 3 oz (80 g) thin sliced pork loin / 1¾ oz (50 g) kimchee / Some scallions / **A** (½ Tbsp soy sauce, 2 tsp sake) / 1 Tbsp sesame oil / 1 serving rice

Method **1.** Rinse kimchee and cut in ¾″ (2 cm) lengths. Cut scallions on an angle into ½″ (1.5 cm) widths. **2.** Sauté pork in sesame oil, add kimchee and scallions and continue to fry and flavor with **A**. Ladle with juice over rice.

Bibinba and Beef Rice Bowl   Kimchee Rice Bowl

69 Mustard Grilled Beef Rice Bowl
(Gyu Karashi-yaki Don)

Liqueur Flavored Kiwi

Ingredients (1 serving) 1 kiwi / 1 tsp cointreau / Some radish

Method Peel kiwi and cut into rounds. Pour cointreau over and chill. Garnish with julienne strips of radish.

Beef cooked with mustard, soy sauce, and sprinkled with sesame seeds. It is easy to make and yet full of flavor. For variety, use vegetables and fruits on hand to make an attractive meal for guests.

Mustard Grilled Beef Rice Bowl

Ingredients (1 serving)   3 oz (80 g) thin sliced beef / **A** (2 Tbsp soy sauce, 1 tsp prepared mustard) / 2 stalks green asparagus / Some each tomatoes and white sesame seeds / 1 serving rice

Method   1. Mix **A** well and marinate beef for 5 minutes.

2. Trim hard root and ends of asparagus, cut in half lengthwise.

3. Place beef and asparagus on a well heated grill. Cook both sides until crispy.

4. Arrange beef and asparagus on hot, steaming rice. Bring remaining marinade to a boil and pour over. Sprinkle toasted sesame seeds, and garnish with tomato.

Vinegared Vegetables

Ingredients (1 serving)   Some celery, carrot, daikon / Flavored vinegar (1 Tbsp vinegar, ¼ tsp sugar, bit soy sauce) / Some white sesame seeds

Method   1. Cut celery, carrots and daikon into julienne strips.

2. Mix flavored vinegar well.

3. Coat vegetables with flavored vinegar and sprinkle with toasted sesame seeds.

Vinegared Rice Bowls

The refreshing acidic taste excites the appetite. Salmon roe, the jewelry of the ocean and the popular tuna. Enjoy using fresh seafood.

70 Scattered Sushi on Rice
(Chirashi Zushi Don)

Ingredients (1 serving)   Desired fish for eating raw (Maine shrimp, porgy, ark shell, squid, tuna, etc.) / ½ sheet toasted nori / 2 leaves green perilla / Some grated wasabi / Soy sauce / 1 serving vinegared rice (see p.55)

Method 1. Choose the freshest fish for raw consumption.
2. Crush nori in hand and scatter over sushi rice. Pile on green perilla and raw fish. Garnish with wasabi to be eaten with soy sauce.

71 Salmon Roe on Rice
(Ikura Don)

Ingredients (1 serving) Some salmon roe / ¼ avocado / ¼ pack daikon sprouts / **A** (1½ Tbsp soy sauce, 1 tsp sake) / 1 serving vinegared rice (see p.55)

Method **1.** Peel avocado and cut into ¼" (5 mm) thin slices and cut into desired shapes with cookie cutters.
2. Cut roots off of daikon sprouts, wash well and drain.
3. Place sprouts on vinegared rice. Arrange avocado and salmon roe colorfully.
4. Mix **A** well and pour over.

72 Raw Tuna on Rice
(Tekka Don)

Ingredients (1 serving) ⅓ block of tuna for raw consumption / 1 sheet toasted nori / **A** (2 Tbsp soy sauce, 1 tsp sake) / Some grated wasabi and cucumber / 1 serving vinegared rice (see p.55)

Method **1.** Cut tuna into thick slices and coat with **A**.
2. Cut half a sheet of nori into ¾" (2 cm) squares and place on vinegared rice. Top with tuna.
3. Pour remainder of **A** over. Cut cucumber into thin rounds, arranging into a container for wasabi. Cut the remaining nori into thin strips and sprinkle over the top.

73 Smoked Salmon on Rice

Ingredients (1 serving) 4 slices smoked salmon / ½ cucumber / Some carrot / 1 leaf lettuce / **A** (1 Tbsp each vinegar and white wine, 2 tsp light soy sauce) / 1 thin slice of lemon / Some capers, canned / 1 serving vinegared rice (next page)

Method **1.** Scrape knobs off of cucumber, wash and slice very thinly lengthwise. Cut carrot into julienne strips.
2. Marinate vegetables and salmon in well mixed **A**.
3. Place torn lettuce on vinegared rice. Top with salmon, vegetables and lemon. Sprinkle with capers.

74 Sardines on Rice
(Iwashi Don)

Ingredients (1 serving) 2 sardines / **A** (1½ Tbsp soy sauce, ½ Tbsp sake, ½ tsp vinegar) / 2 leaves green perilla / 1 chive / Some ginger / 1 Tbsp white sesame seeds / 1 serving vinegared rice (next page)

Method **1.** Cut sardine in three pieces (see page 24). Remove skin. Slice in half and coat with **A**.
2. Place green perilla on vinegared rice. Lay sardines on top. Sprinkle with chives chopped in rounds and toasted sesame seeds.
3. Garnish with needle thin slivers of ginger.

How to Make Vinegared Rice

When making vinegared rice to serve with seafood,
reduce the sweetness for a refreshing taste.

POINT

1. Use the same amount of rice and water and cook into firm rice.
2. Add flavored vinegar before the rice cools.
3. To avoid the rice becoming sticky, mix with a cutting motion.
4. Using a fan quickly brings out a shiny surface.

1. To prevent rice from sticking to the wooden bowl, dampen by wiping with a moistened dishcloth.

2. Cook 2 cups of rice with 2 cups water. Let steam shorter than usual. Insert a spatula between the rice and pan and rotate around the pan.

3. Hold the pan in both hands and turn over in one motion to transfer rice to wooden bowl.

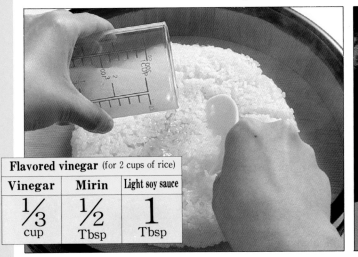

Flavored vinegar (for 2 cups of rice)		
Vinegar	Mirin	Light soy sauce
1/3 cup	1/2 Tbsp	1 Tbsp

4. Pour flavored vinegar over all in one circular motion. Use spatula quickly to mix.

5. Once the vinegar is well absorbed, make large cutting motions in rice, turning rice and mix while fanning.

Easy Microwave Directions

Pouring flavored vinegar over cold cooked rice and heating is an easy way to make vinegared rice.

Method (1 serving)   **1.** Wrap 1 cup cold rice and heat in microwave for 1 minute 30 seconds.
2. Using a third of the flavored vinegar above, pour over, around and quickly cut into rice to mix.

Buttered Rice and Turmeric Rice Dishes

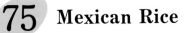

75 Mexican Rice

Ingredients (1 serving)   1¾ oz (50 g) ground beef / ½ each red and green peppers / ¼ onion / Some celery / **A** (3 Tbsp tomato puree, ¼ cup soup stock, some each tabasco, granulated soup bouillon, black pepper, powdered chili pepper) / 1 egg / 1 Tbsp oil for sautéing / Some parsley / 1 serving buttered rice (see next page)

Method   **1.** Remove core and seeds from peppers. Mince peppers, onion and celery.
2. Heat oil and sauté beef and vegetables until beef flaked. Add **A** and simmer 4~5 minutes.
3. Cover egg with water and boil 15 minutes to make boiled egg.
4. Ladle beef and vegetables over buttered rice. Garnish with the egg in halves and parsley.

76 Ham and Egg on Rice

Ingredients (1 serving)   3~4 pieces ham / 1 egg / 4 snow peas / ½ Tbsp oil for frying / 1 serving turmeric rice (see next page)

Method **1.** Heat oil in a fry pan, arrange ham overlapping to a circle. Crack egg in the center. Cover pan and cook to desired degree.
2. Place on turmeric rice. Garnish with parboiled snow peas. Add worcester sauce.

Use buttered rice for modern Western dishes and flavored turmeric rice for seafood dishes. Either one creates a fresh, vivid colored chic dish. Enjoy making rice dishes with these varieties.

Making Buttered Rice

Ingredients (3~4 servings)

2 cups rice

2 Tbsp butter

2 cups soup stock

⅓ tsp salt

Some pepper

▶ 30 minutes before cooking, wash rice, place in colander and set aside. When covered, cook on medium low until the steam disappears. Finish on low.

1. Melt butter in a heavy pan over a low flame taking care not to burn.

2. Add well-drained rice, and sauté while stirring with a wooden spatula.

3. Sauté carefully until the grains of rice become shiny.

4. Add preheated soup stock, salt and pepper and stir together. Cover with a lid.

5. Cook for 12 minutes. Turn off heat and steam for 13 minutes.

Making Turmeric Rice

Ingredients (3~4 servings)

2 cups rice

2 Tbsp butter

1 tsp turmeric

2 cups hot water

Method **1.** Wash rice, place in colander for 30 minutes.
2. Heat pan, melt butter and sauté rice well.
3. Then, shake turmeric in, spreading while sautéing. (photo 1)
4. Add hot water and mix. Cook as for buttered rice.

(photo 2) It yields a beautiful, golden rice. (photo 3)

Turmeric contains a yellow color. It is used in curry powder and prepared mustard. It also has a slight fragrance. Sold in powdered form.

77 Chicken in White Sauce on Rice

Ingredients (1 serving)   3 oz (80 g) chicken breast / ¼ onion / 3 Tbsp frozen mixed vegetables / ⅓ cup water / ½ cup milk / Some granulated soup bouillon / Pinch salt and pepper / 1 Tbsp oil for sautéing / 1 tsp cornstarch diluted in water / 1 serving buttered rice (see p.57)

Method 1. Cut chicken into ¾" (2 cm) cubes and onion into ½" (1.5 cm) cubes. Let vegetables come to room temperature and rinse.

2. Heat oil in a pan and sauté chicken and onions. When the chicken turns white, add vegetables and sauté quickly.

3. Add measured water and soup bouillon. Bring to a boil. Add milk, bring to a boil, season with salt and pepper. Thicken with cornstarch diluted in water.

4. Prepare butter rice as on page 57, and ladle chicken with white sauce over all.

78 Italian Rice

Ingredients (1 serving)   1¾ oz (50 g) sliced beef / ¼ onion / ½ green pepper / Some celery / ½ small can sliced mushrooms / **A** (⅓ cup soup stock, 3 Tbsp canned demi-glaze sauce, 1 Tbsp red wine) / Salt / Pepper / 1 Tbsp oil for sautéing / Some broccoli / 1 serving buttered rice

Method 1. Cut beef into bite sized pieces. Sprinkle with salt and pepper.

2. Cut onion thinly. Remove core and seeds from green

79 Dry Curried Beef on Rice

Ingredients (1 serving)   1¾ oz (50 g) ground beef / ¼ onion / 1 small green pepper / ½ small can sliced mushrooms / 1 Tbsp raisins / ½ Tbsp curry powder / Pinch salt and pepper / 1 Tbsp oil for sautéing / 1 pickle / 1 serving turmeric rice (see p. 57)

Method **1.** Coarsely chop onion. Remove core and seeds from green pepper. Cut into ⅜″ (1 cm) wide pieces. Soak raisins in weak tea until soft, but retaining their flavor.

2. Heat oil in a fry pan. Sauté onions until sweet. Add beef and sauté together until broken up.

3. Add drained raisins and mushrooms and sauté briefly, sprinkle curry powder over and sauté in. Finally, add green pepper, sauté together and flavor with salt and pepper.

4. Place (3) on turmeric rice and garnish with thinly, sliced pickles.

pepper and slice thinly. Remove strings from celery and slice in thin strips.

3. Heat oil in a pan and sauté beef quickly, add vegetables and mushrooms and sauté.

4. Add **A** and simmer 4~5 minutes. Season with salt and pepper.

5. Make buttered rice as on page 57. Pour beef mixture over and garnish colorfully with broccoli parboiled in salted water.

80 Corned Beef on Rice

Ingredients (1 serving)   1¾ oz (50 g) canned corned beef / ¼ onion / ½ stalk broccoli (¼ American size) / 1 Tbsp white wine / Pinch salt and pepper / 1 Tbsp oil for sautéing / 1 serving buttered rice

Method **1.** Remove corned beef from can. Using a fork, break apart.
2. Cut onion into ¼″ (7 mm) wide thin slices. Break broccoli into pieces and parboil in salted water until bright green.
3. Heat oil in fry pan, sauté onion until soft. Add corned beef and quickly sauté together. Add broccoli and sauté together once more.
4. Sprinkle with white wine, lightly salt and pepper to season. Serve on top of buttered rice.

81 Eggplant and Bacon on Rice

Ingredients (1 serving)   1 eggplant / 2 slices bacon / ¼ onion / **A** (2 tsp red wine, ½ Tbsp curry powder, ¼ cup soup stock, pinch salt and pepper) / Some oil for sautéing / Oil for deep frying / 1 serving buttered rice

Method **1.** Remove cap from eggplant and cut into ⅜″ (1 cm) rounds. Soak in water to remove harshness. Pat dry thoroughly.
2. Cut onion into half moons and separate rings. Cut bacon into 1½″ (4 cm) wide pieces.
3. Deep fry eggplant and onion in 340°F (170°C) oil or sauté until well browned.
4. Sauté bacon, until crispy, in fry pan with no extra oil added.
5. Heat oil in pan, add vegetables and bacon and then **A**. Mix quickly, seasoning and serve on buttered rice.

82 Wieners on Rice

Ingredients (1 serving)   5 sausage wieners / ¼ onion / 4 mushrooms, canned / **A** (2 Tbsp tomato ketchup, 1 tsp worcester sauce, some soy sauce, 3 Tbsp soup stock) / 1 Tbsp oil for sautéing / Some minced parsley / 1 serving buttered rice

Method 1. Use a knife to slice a grid on the surface of the wiener.

2. Cut onion thinly, and the mushrooms in half.

3. Heat oil in a fry pan. Sauté wieners and onions. When the onions softened, add mushrooms.

4. Add **A** seasoning and soup. Mix and bring to a boil.

5. Ladle over buttered rice. Garnish with parsley.

83 Orange Simmered Spareribs on Rice

Ingredients (2 servings)   8 spareribs / Simmering stock (2 Tbsp low sugar orange marmalade, 2 Tbsp each soy sauce and sake, ⅓ cup water) / Some chervil / 2 servings turmeric rice

Method 1. Boil spareribs in plenty of water for 30 minutes, skimming off any scum.

2. Place simmering stock ingredients and spareribs in a heavy pan and bring to a boil. Simmer 30 minutes until meat almost separates from the bones.

3. Place spareribs on top of turmeric rice and garnish with chervil.

84 Octopus Simmered in Tomato Sauce on Rice

Ingredients (1 serving) 5¼ oz (150 g) boiled octopus / Tomato sauce (½ cup canned boiled tomatoes, 1 small clove garlic, pinch salt, pepper and sugar, some granulated soup bouillon) / 2 tsp oil for sautéing / Some potato starch diluted in water / Some minced parsley / 1 serving buttered rice

Method **1.** Cut boiled octopus roughly into bite sized cubes.

2. To make tomato sauce, mince garlic and sauté in a well heated, oiled pan until fragrant. Add canned tomatoes (including liquid) and bring to a boil while breaking up. Add seasoning and soup bouillon and bring to a boil again. Adjust flavor.

3. Add octopus to sauce and simmer for some time. Thicken with potato starch diluted in water to finish.

4. Ladle over buttered rice and garnish with plenty of parsley.

85

Wine Simmered Chicken on Rice

Ingredients (1 serving) 3½ oz (100g) chicken breast / 1 strip bacon / ¼ onion / **A** (¼ cup red wine, 2 tsp soy sauce, pinch sugar) / 1 Tbsp oil for sautéing / Some parsley / 1 serving buttered rice

Method **1.** Cut chicken in half and pierce skin with a fork to aid in flavor ab-

86 Chicken Nuggets on Rice

Ingredients (1 serving)   3½ oz (100 g) chicken thigh / 1/4 onion / Sauce (3 Tbsp canned demi-glaze sauce, 1 Tbsp red wine, 3 Tbsp soup stock, pinch salt and pepper, 1/3 tsp sugar) / Salt, Pepper, Flour / Some parsley / Oil for frying / 1 serving turmeric rice

Method

1. Cut chicken into bite sized pieces, sprinkle lightly with salt and pepper and roll in flour. Cut onion in ⅜″ (1 cm) wide rounds and separate into rings.

2. Preheat oil to 350°F (175°C), deep fry onions. Next, fry chicken until crispy, brown.

3. Place sauce ingredients in a small pan and simmer, stirring constantly with spatula for 2 minutes.

4. Arrange chicken and onions on rice and pour sauce around over all. Sprinkle well with minced parsley.

sorption.

2. Cut bacon into 3 pieces. Mince onion coarsely.

3. Heat oil in fry pan, add onions and bacon and sauté well. Add chicken and cook until crispy and browned.

4. Add **A** and cook chicken through over low heat.

5. Ladle chicken mixture over buttered rice and garnish with parsley.

87 Pork Simmered in Tomato Sauce on Rice

Ingredients (1 serving) 1¾ oz (50 g) sliced pork shank / 1 each small green and yellow peppers / ¼ can canned tomato / ½ cup soup stock / 1 Tbsp each red wine and tomato ketchup / Salt and pepper / 1 Tbsp oil for sautéing / 1 serving turmeric rice

Method **1.** Cut pork into bite sized pieces. Sprinkle lightly with salt and pepper. Cut peppers in thick rounds, removing core and seeds.

2. Heat oil in pan and sauté pork. When the pork changes color, add peppers and sauté quickly.

3. Add canned tomatoes and soup, stir with spatula while simmering for 2~3 minutes.

4. When meat and vegetables are cooked through, add wine, ketchup and a pinch of salt and pepper to flavor. Simmer for 2~3 minutes and serve over rice.

88 Sardines in Oil on Rice

Ingredients (1 serving) 2½ oz (70 g) sardines in oil, canned / 4 small stalks green asparagus / 1 Tbsp butter / 2 Tbsp soy sauce / 2 tsp sake / Some red pickled ginger / 1 serving buttered rice

Method **1.** Remove sardines from can and drain off the oil.

2. Trim the hard ends from asparagus and cut them in half lengthwise.

3. Melt butter. Sauté asparagus and sardines, in that order. Add soy sauce and sake. Coat all.

4. Pile on buttered rice. Pour remaining liquid over and garnish with pickled ginger.

89 Beef Stroganoff on Rice

Ingredients (1 serving) 3 oz (80 g) sliced beef / 2 mushrooms / ¼ onion / ½ clove garlic / 1 Tbsp butter / ½ Tbsp flour / ⅔ cup soup stock / 1/4 cup tomato puree / Some paprika / 1 Tbsp heavy cream / 1 Tbsp red wine / Pinch sugar / Salt and pepper / 1 serving turmeric rice

Method **1.** Cut beef into ⅜" (1 cm) wide pieces.

2. Slice mushrooms thinly, onions into ⅜" (1 cm) wide wedges. Mince garlic.

3. Melt butter in a heavy pan and sauté garlic. When fragrant, add beef and sauté. Next, add onions and mushrooms and sauté over high heat.

4. When vegetables soften, sprinkle with flour and mix well.

5. Add tomato puree, mix and pour in soup. When it comes to a boil, carefully remove all the froth from the surface and sprinkle with paprika. Cook over low heat.

6. When the flavor has cooked in, about 6 minutes, add wine, sugar, salt and pepper to flavor. When done, add heavy cream.

7. Bring to a boil and ladle generously over turmeric rice.

90 Hamburger on Rice

Ingredients (1 serving)   1¾ oz (50 g) ground beef / 1 oz (30 g) ground pork / 2 Tbsp bread crumbs / 1 Tbsp soup stock / ¼ small onion / ⅓ small egg / 1½ oz (40 g) frozen mixed vegetables / Salt and pepper / Some nutmeg / 2 Tbsp oil for frying / Some tomato ketchup and tat soy / 1 serving buttered rice

Method   **1.** Mix bread crumbs and soup. Mince onion and sauté with 1 tsp oil until browned and fragrant.

2. Place ground beef and pork in a bowl and mix. Blend in salt, pepper and nutmeg. Add beaten egg and (1), and mix together until it becomes sticky. Separate in two, toss from one hand to the other to release air. Shape into ovals, depressing center slightly to aid in cooking through.

3. Heat 1 Tbsp oil in a fry pan, brown on both sides over high heat, cover and cook on low heat until middle is cooked.

4. Sauté frozen vegetables straight from the freezer in 2 tsp oil, lightly sprinkle with salt and pepper to flavor.

5. Arrange mixed vegetables and hamburger on buttered rice, add tomato ketchup and garnish with tat soy.

91 Spanish Rice

Ingredients (1 serving) 2 scallops / ¼ cuttlefish / ½ each red and green peppers / Some yellow pepper / 2 thin slices lemon / 1 Tbsp white wine / **A** (½ cup soup stock, some saffron, pinch salt and pepper) / 2 Tbsp oil for sautéing / 1 serving buttered rice

Method **1.** Cut scallop in half on a slight angle. Remove legs and innards from cuttlefish and cut in rings. Parboil.

2. Remove core and seeds from peppers and cut using a rolling cut into wedges.

3. Heat oil in a pan, add scallops, cuttlefish, peppers, lemon and sauté.

4. When seafood cooked through, sprinkle white wine over, add **A** and simmer for 2 minutes.

5. Ladle all, including liquid, over buttered rice. Squeeze lemon over if desired.

▶ Substitute seafood such as shrimp, octopus, or mussels, as desired.

Saffron Rice Dishes

Great with seafood!!
Dishes using vivid, golden color saffron rice.

Making Saffron Rice

Ingredients (3~4 servings)
2 cups rice
2 cups hot water
⅓ tsp saffron

Saffron
The dried flower pistils are expensive. They have their own fragrance and when soaked in water yield a beautiful golden color.

1. Cover saffron with hot water, set aside until colorful.

2. Wash rice and drain in a colander for 30 minutes.

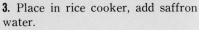

3. Place in rice cooker, add saffron water.

4. Cook as usual.

5. Fragrant, golden saffron rice is ready!

92 Grilled Jumbo Shrimp on Rice

Ingredients (1 serving) 2 jumbo shrimp / Some each yellow and green pepper / 1 Tbsp each soy sauce and sake / Some chervil / 1 serving saffron rice (this page)
Method **1.** Cut legs from shrimp. Using a knife, cut

93 Shrimp Fritters on Rice

Ingredients (1 serving) 8 shrimp / Batter (½ egg yolk, ½ egg white, 2~3 drops vegetable oil, 2 Tbsp each water and flour) / Some tomato sauce (store bought) / Oil for frying / Some flour / Some watercress / 1 serving saffron rice

Method **1.** Devein and shell shrimp.
2. Place egg yolk, vegetable oil and water in a bowl and mix. Sprinkle flour on and lightly mix. Beat egg white, add to above and fold in to finish batter.
3. Lightly sprinkle shrimp with flour. Cover with batter and fry until crispy in 350˚F (175˚C) oil.
4. Arrange shrimp and watercress on saffron rice and pour tomato sauce over.

from head to tail along the back to open. Remove innards.
2. Cut peppers in thin rings.
3. Preheat grill well, place shrimp on the grill. Mix soy sauce and sake. Brush over while cooking through. Grill peppers quickly.
4. Arrange shrimp and green peppers on saffron rice colorfully. Pour remaining soy sauce and sake mixture over and garnish with chervil.

Entertaining with Rice Dishes

Using mussels or desired seafood, such as cuttlefish or shrimp, this western style rice dish is chic. We used buttered rice (p.57). By adding soup and vegetables, this becomes a fun dish to serve guests at lunch.

94 Mussels Rice Bowl

Ingredients (1 serving)   5 mussels in the shell / 1 shallot / 2~3 canned mushrooms / 1 tsp Madeira wine / 2 Tbsp evaporated milk / ⅔ cup boiling water / Pinch salt, pepper, sugar / 1 Tbsp oil for sautéing / 1 serving buttered rice (p. 57)

Method 1. Wash mussels well with a brush. Boil in ⅔ cup boiling water with salt added. Cut shallot into round thin slices and mushrooms thinly.
2. Heat oil in fry pan and sauté shallot. Add mushrooms and sprinkle with Madeira wine.
3. Add mussels and the boiled water, bring to a boil and pour in milk. Season with salt, pepper and sugar.
4. Ladle mussels mixture over rice.

Egg Soup

Ingredients (1 serving)   ½ beaten egg / Some each green and red pepper / 1 leaf lettuce / **A** (1 cup water, some granulated soup bouillon, salt, pepper, sugar)
Method 1. Remove core and seeds from pepper and cut into thin rings. Wash lettuce and tear into easy to eat pieces.
2. Place **A** in a pan, add vegetables and bring to a boil.
3. Pour beaten egg into soup through a perforated ladle. When half cooked turn off heat.

Vegetable Sticks

Ingredients (1 serving)   Some cucumber, celery, carrot, pickles and red pickled ginger
Method   Cut vegetables into 3¼″ (8 cm) sticks and arrange with pickles and pickled ginger.

Miniature Rice Bowls

They will be welcomed by those lacking appetite or for accompanying alcoholic beverages.
Use rice bowls with diameters of roughly 4″ (10 cm).

Cod Roe Rice Bowl

Fried Tofu Sheet on Rice

Pickled Plum Rice Bowl

95 Fried Tofu Sheet on Rice
(Kitsune Don)

Ingredients (1 serving)   1 slice aburage (fried tofu sheet) / 1 clove ginger / Simmering stock (½ cup dashi stock, 1½ Tbsp soy sauce, 2 tsp sugar, 1 tsp each sake and mirin) / 1 serving rice

Method   1. Cut aburage in two, place in a colander and pour boiling water over to wash away excess oil

2. Cut ginger into julienne strips.

3. Place simmering stock in a pan and bring to a boil, add aburage and ginger and simmer to aborb the flavor. (Only a little liquid remains.)

4. Place (3) including remaining liquid on hot rice.

96 Cod Roe Rice Bowl
(Tarako no Ama-kara Don)

Ingredients (1 serving)   1 raw cod roe pod / Simmering stock (½ cup water, ¼ cup soy sauce, 3 Tbsp sugar, 2 Tbsp sake) / Some chives / 1 serving rice

Method   1. Bring simmering stock to a boil and add cod roe. Simmer over low until flavor is saturated.

2. Cut into bite sized pieces and place on hot, steaming rice. Garnish with chives cut into rings.

97 Pickled Plum Rice Bowl
(Bai Niku Don)

Ingredients (1 serving)   ½ sheet tatami-iwashi (baby sar-

Yamato-ni Beef on Rice

Vinegared Porgy on Rice

dines dried into a sheet) / 1 leaf green perilla / 1 tsp pickled plum (umeboshi) / Soy sauce / 1 serving rice

Method **1.** Cut tatami-iwashi into easy to eat pieces. Place on a grill and quickly broil.

2. Place perilla on rice and top with tatami-iwashi and pickled plum. Pour desired amount of soy sauce over.

98 Yamato-ni Beef on Rice

Ingredients (1 serving)   3~4 slices canned Yamato-ni beef / ¼ onion / **A** (3 Tbsp vinegar, ½ Tbsp vegetable oil, pinch salt and sugar) / Pinch salt / 1 serving rice

Method **1.** Cut onion very thinly, sprinkle with a pinch of salt and knead. When softened, rinse and squeeze out moisture.

2. Mix **A** ingredients together well and mix with onion.

3. Place beef and onions on hot, steaming rice.

99 Vinegared Porgy on Rice

Ingredients (1 serving)   4 cuts small vinegared porgy (store bought) / Shredded omelet (1 egg, pinch sugar and salt, some oil for frying) / Sauce (2 tsp soy sauce, some grated wasabi) / Some kinome / 1 serving rice

Method **1.** Beat egg, flavor with sugar and salt. Fry to make omelet. Roll up and cut into thin strips to make shredded omelet.

2. Place omelet strips and porgy on hot, steaming rice. Mix sauce and pour over. Garnish with kinome.

Miniature Bowls
of Glutinous Rice

This rice bowl should be eaten hot and steaming. Make from ingredients from sea and mountain.

Steamed Sea Urchin Rice Bowl

Gifts from the Mountain Rice Bowl

100 Steamed Sea Urchin Rice Bowl

Ingredients (1 serving)   Steamed sea urchin (store bought) / 3 ginko nuts / Some toasted nori / **A** (1 Tbsp soy sauce, ½ Tbsp sake) / Pinch salt / 1 serving glutinous rice (see next page)

Method **1.** Crack open ginko nut and remove from shell. Parboil in slightly salted water and remove thin inner peel. Slice thinly. **2.** Place steamed sea urchin and ginko nuts on glutinous rice. Mix **A** well and pour it over. Steam for 5 minutes. **3.** Sprinkle toasted nori slivers over while piping hot.

101 Adductor of Round Clam Rice Bowl

Ingredients (1 serving)   1 oz (30 g) adductor of round clam / Some thinly sliced honewort / **A** (2 tsp soy sauce, some sake) / 1 serving glutinous rice

Method **1.** Wash adductor quickly in salted water and drain. Place on glutinous rice and sprinkle with honewort. **2.** Mix **A** and pour over. Steam for 5 minutes.

102 Gifts from the Mountain Rice Bowl

Ingredients (1 serving)   2 chestnuts / 2 small dried shiitake mushrooms / Simmering stock (¼ cup dashi stock, 1½ Tbsp soy sauce, 1 Tbsp sugar) / 1 serving glutinous rice

Method **1.** Boil chestnut and remove both outer shell and inner peel. **2.** Reconstitute shiitake in warm water. Remove hard end of stem. Simmer in stock. Slice into thin pieces. **3.** Place chestnut and shiitake on glutinous rice and steam for 5 minutes.

74

White Bait Rice Bowl

Kombu Tsukudani on Rice

103 White Bait Rice Bowl

Ingredients (1 serving)   1 oz (30 g) white bait / ½ egg / Simmering stock (⅓ cup dashi stock, ½ Tbsp each light soy sauce and sake) / 1 serving glutinous rice

Method   **1.** Bring simmering stock to a boil, add white bait and simmer for a short time.

2. Beat egg, pour in quickly and turn off heat when half done.

3. Pour the whole over hot, steaming glutinous rice.

104 Kombu Tsukudani on Rice

Ingredients (1 serving)   1 Tbsp kombu tsukudani / ½ slice bacon / Some chives / 1 serving glutinous rice

Method   **1.** Slice bacon thinly and place in a fry pan and sauté until crispy.

2. Cut chives into rings.

3. Place tsukudani and bacon on rice and sprinkle chives colorfully.

Making Glutinous Rice

Boiling - Wash glutinous rice well, place in a colander and drain. Place in inside pan of rice cooker. Use 20% less water than for regular rice.

Steaming - Soak glutinous rice overnight. Place in colander. Preheat steamer placing a wet towel in. When steam appears, place rice inside and steam over high for 20 minutes. During steaming, sprinkle water by hand 2~3 times for fluffy rice.

Vinegared Dishes

to Accompany Rice Bowls

Refreshing acidity and pleasing texture. Rice dishes which are often sweet and salty go well with vinegared dishes.

Pickled Vegetables with Vinegar

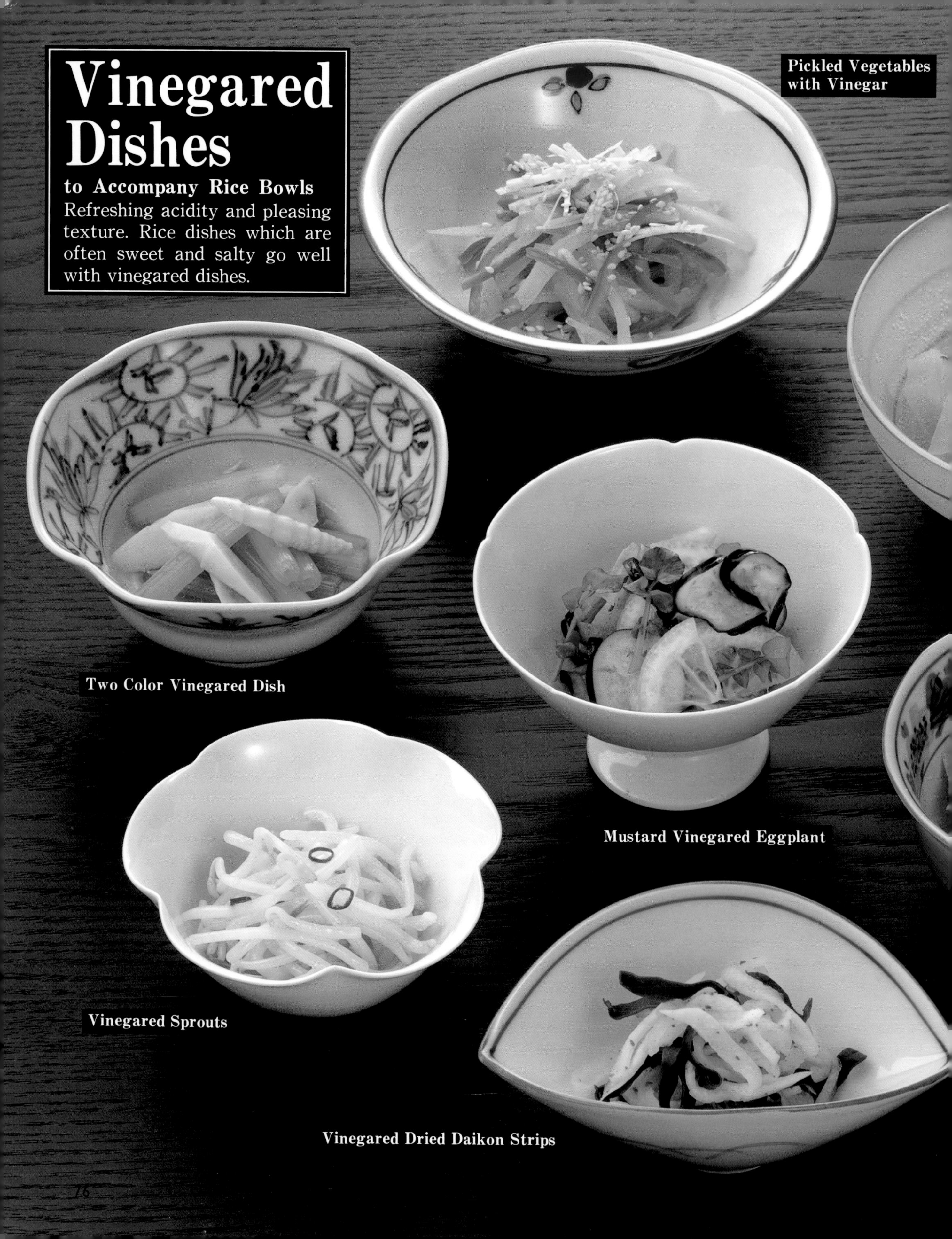

Two Color Vinegared Dish

Mustard Vinegared Eggplant

Vinegared Sprouts

Vinegared Dried Daikon Strips

Vinegared Turnip

Vinegared Cabbage

Two Color Vinegared Dish

Ingredients (2~3 servings)   2 stalks coltsfoot / 1 can boiled bamboo shoot hearts (store bought) / Sweet vinegar (½ cup vinegar, 3 Tbsp sugar, 2 Tbsp light soy sauce) / Salt
Method   1. Cut coltsfoot into 3 pieces each, sprinkle with salt and roll on cutting board. Boil for 2 minutes. Remove to ice water and peel. Cut into 1⅛″ (3 cm) pieces. **2.** Cut bamboo hearts into 1⅛″ (3 cm) slices on an angle. **3.** Mix sweet vinegar well and coat coltsfoot and bamboo hearts.

Vinegared Sprouts

Ingredients (2~3 servings)   7 oz (200 g) soybean sprouts / 1 red chili pepper / Sweet vinegar (⅓ cup vinegar, ½ tsp salt, 1 Tbsp sugar, some sesame oil) / Some vinegar
Method   1. Remove root end of sprouts and rinse. Parboil in vinegared water. Remove to a colander to cool. **2.** Remove seeds from pepper and cut into tiny rings. **3.** Mix sweet vinegar well, add pepper and coat sprouts.

Pickled Vegetables with Vinegar

Ingredients (2~3 servings)   ⅓ takuan (daikon pickled in rice bran) / 1 green pepper / 1 small knob ginger / Sweet vinegar (¼ cup vinegar, 1 Tbsp light soy sauce, pinch sugar) / Some white sesame seeds
Method   1. Cut takuan into 1⅛″ (3 cm) long julienne strips, wash and squeeze out water. **2.** Remove core and seeds from green pepper. Cut, along with ginger, into julienne strips. **3.** Mix takuan and vegetables, coat with sweet vinegar. Arrange on a plate and sprinkle with sesame seeds.

Mustard Vinegared Eggplant

Ingredients (2~3 servings)   2 eggplants / 3~4 pieces watercress / Slice lemon / Mustard vinegar (¼ cup vinegar, 1 tsp sugar, ½ Tbsp soy sauce, 1 tsp prepared mustard) / Pinch salt
Method   1. Remove cap from eggplant and cut into thin rounds. Sprinkle with salt and knead lightly. **2.** Cut off hard stem of watercress. Cut lemon slices into 4 pieces. **3.** Squeeze moisture from eggplant, put together with watercress and lemon and coat with mustard vinegar.

Vinegared Dried Daikon Strips

Ingredients (2~3 servings)   ¾ oz (20 g) dried daikon strips / ⅜ oz (10 g) thinly cut kombu / Vinegar dressing (2 Tbsp vinegar, 1½ Tbsp soy sauce, ½ Tbsp sake, powdered chili pepper)
Method   1. Place dried daikon in water, kneading and changing water 2~3 times. Soak again in plenty of water for 5 minutes to reconstitute. **2.** Place in colander, pour boiling water over and squeeze out liquid. **3.** Reconstitute kombu by soaking in water for 3 minutes. **4.** Mix vinegar dressing ingredients well and coat the daikon strips and kombu.

Vinegared Turnip

Ingredients (2~3 servings)   2 turnips / 2 rings canned pineapple / 3 radishes / Vinegar dressing (¼ cup each wine vinegar and vegetable oil, ½ tsp salt, dash pepper) / Some lettuce
Method   1. Slice turnip into thin wedges and parboil. **2.** Cut each pineapple ring into 8 pieces, radish into thin wedges and tear lettuce into bite size. **3.** Coat all with vinegar dressing.

Vinegared Cabbage

Ingredients (2~3 servings)   5 leaves cabbage / ½ red onion / Vinegar dressing (¼ cup vinegar, 1 Tbsp vegetable oil) / 1 tsp salt
Method   1. Remove thick ridge of cabbage. Cut into julienne strips. Slice red onion thinly. **2.** Place in bowl, sprinkle with salt and knead until pliant. Rinse. **3.** Squeeze out water and coat with vinegar dressing.

Side Dishes
for Rice Bowls

Three Colored Sauté

Vegetables Simmered in Soup

Simmered Wakame

Soy Dressed Vegetables

Quickly Sautéed Vegetables

Adding a more involved dish such as simmered or sautéed dishes makes for a thoughtful dinner.

Sautéed and Simmered Hijiki

Flavored Turnip Greens

Simmered Wakame

Ingredients (2~3 servings)   1 oz (30 g) reconstituted wakame (⅛ oz/3 g dried) / ½ cup dried small shrimp / Simmering stock (⅔ cup dashi stock, 1 Tbsp soy sauce, 1 tsp sake)

Method 1. Reconstitute wakame in water for 5 minutes, squeeze out water and cut into bite sized pieces.

2. Place stock ingredients in a small pan, bring to a boil, add wakame and shrimp and boil briefly.

Quickly Sautéed Vegetables

Ingredients (2~3 servings)   2 slices bacon / 1¾ oz (50 g) string beans / ½ onion / Pinch salt and pepper / 2 tsp oil for frying

Method 1. Cut each bacon into 3 pieces. Remove strings from string beans and snap in half. Cut onion in ⅜" (1 cm) wide slices.

2. Heat oil in fry pan, sauté bacon and vegetables. Flavor with salt and pepper.

Three Colored Sauté

Ingredients (2~3 servings)   1 potato / 1 green pepper / Some carrot / 1 Tbsp light soy sauce / 2 tsp sake / Dash pepper / 2 tsp oil for sautéing

Method 1. Cut potato and carrot into 2" (5 cm) long julienne strips. Remove core and seeds from green pepper and cut thinly.

2. Heat oil in fry pan, add vegetables and sauté over high, stopping while they are still crunchy.

3. Add soy sauce, sake and pepper and mix quickly to flavor.

Vegetables Simmered in Soup

Ingredients (2~3 servings)   1 carrot / 8 mini onions / 1 small stalk broccoli / 1½ cup soup stock / 1 tsp vegetable oil / Pinch salt and pepper

Method 1. Cut carrot and trim into balls the size of the onions. Cut in half. Cut the onions in half. Separate broccoli into flowerets.

2. Place vegetables and soup in a pan. Add vegetable oil, salt and pepper. Simmer over low heat until softened.

Soy Dressed Vegetables

Ingredients (2~3 servings)   ½ stalk celery / ¼ carrot / 1 cucumber (½ American size) / 2 tsp soy sauce / 1 Tbsp sake / Some white sesame seeds / Some salt

Method 1. Remove strings from celery. Sprinkle cucumber with salt, roll on a cutting board and rinse. Cut all vegetables into 2" (5 cm) long julienne strips.

2. Mix soy sauce and sake and coat vegetables well.

3. Arrange on a plate and sprinkle white sesame lightly.

Sautéed and Simmered Hijiki

Ingredients (2~3 servings)   1¾ oz (50 g) reconstituted hijiki seaweed (⅜ oz/10 g dried) / 1 stick chikuwa (fish paste tube) / Simmering stock (⅓ cup dashi stock, 2 Tbsp soy sauce, 2 tsp sugar) / 1 Tbsp sesame oil

Method 1. Drain hijiki and cut long pieces into easy to eat lengths. Cut chikuwa into bite sized pieces.

2. Sautée hijiki in sesame oil. When hijiki is covered with oil, add chikuwa and quickly sauté.

3. Add stock and simmer for 7~8 minutes.

Flavored Turnip Greens

Ingredients (2~3 servings)   Greens from 2 turnips / 3 ark shells (for raw consumption) / 2 tsp soy sauce / Pinch sugar / Salt / Vinegar

Method 1. Cut turnip greens into ¾" (2 cm) lengths. Parboil in salted water.

2. Knead meat of ark shell with a little salt, rinse. Slice a grid on the surface. Sprinkle with vinegar and do a vinegar wash.

3. Mix soy sauce, pinch sugar and salt. Coat turnip greens and ark shell.

INDEX by Ingredients